One More Play

Dr. James M Perdue

WestBow
PRESS
A DIVISION OF THOMAS NELSON

Copyright © 2012 Dr. James Perdue

All rights reserved. No part of this book may be used or reproduced by any means, graphic, electronic, or mechanical, including photocopying, recording, taping or by any information storage retrieval system without the written permission of the publisher except in the case of brief quotations embodied in critical articles and reviews.

WestBow Press books may be ordered through booksellers or by contacting:

WestBow Press
A Division of Thomas Nelson
1663 Liberty Drive
Bloomington, IN 47403
www.westbowpress.com
1-(866) 928-1240

Because of the dynamic nature of the Internet, any web addresses or links contained in this book may have changed since publication and may no longer be valid. The views expressed in this work are solely those of the author and do not necessarily reflect the views of the publisher, and the publisher hereby disclaims any responsibility for them.

Any people depicted in stock imagery provided by Thinkstock are models, and such images are being used for illustrative purposes only.

Certain stock imagery © Thinkstock.

ISBN: 978-1-4497-6868-3 (sc)
ISBN: 978-1-4497-6869-0 (e)
ISBN: 978-1-4497-6870-6 (hc)

Library of Congress Control Number: 2012917792
Printed in the United States of America

WestBow Press rev. date: 10/10/2012

Contents

Chapter 1. The Family that Perseveres 1
Chapter 2. Invincible 11
Chapter 3. What Am I To Do With My Life? 23
Chapter 4. Spain, I Can't Speak Spanish 41
Chapter 5. Readjusting to Home Life 51
Chapter 6. I Can't Quit My Education Now 75
Chapter 7. It's Off to Work I Go 83
Chapter 8. The Price of Glory is High 93
Chapter 9. Happy Birthday to Me 99
Chapter 10. I'm Going Where? 109
Chapter 11. Anjouan, Here We Come 127
Chapter 12. The Beginning of the End 141
Chapter 13. Good Bye, Andy 149
Chapter 14. Strike Three – You're Not Out 161
Chapter 15. There's No Need To Fear – Ricardo Is Here 177

One More Play

Ricardo says, "Thank you."

Dedication

Thank you goes to Mom and my brothers, Tim and Andy. I know I wouldn't be where I am in life, if God hadn't blessed me with all of you as my family. This life has been a long hard road, but you have provided me with the needed support, love, and discipline to become successful.

Acknowledgement

THANK YOU GOD for continually putting, *One More Play*, on my heart so I would finish. I hope the reader can take some hope and inspiration from the reading and use it to accomplish the desires of their hearts. For everybody reading, *One More Play*, thank you for the times you encourage others and provide hope in their lives. Remember, hope comes in many different forms.

Thanks to many people from different groups, such as Hendersonville Toastmasters, Heart to Heart Storytellers of Hendersonville, especially Bob and Jane, and Canine Companion for Independence – for continually encouraging my dream: to finish this book. Thank you for my editors and readers, Brenda, Cindy, Jane, Jessye, Kay (s), Marjorie and Shirley for finding my mistakes. You made the reading more fluent. Thank you, Dwayne for shooting the front cover and Le Print Express thank you for the author's picture.

An enormous thanks to my friends who have supported, prayed, and loved me during my road from failure to success.

Special thanks to Barbra, Beth, Heather, Pam, Rose and Tom. All of you have been there during my times of need to help support and encourage me. I appreciate your friendship and love. Dr. Case and staff, thank you for keeping me healthy throughout all these years.

Some names have been changed to protect their privacy.

Introduction

Difficulties are meant to rouse, not discourage. The human spirit is to grow strong by conflict.
William Ellery Channing

PAUL "BEAR" BRYANT, who coached football at the University of Alabama, once said, "It's not the will to win that matters. Everyone has that. It's the will to prepare to win that matters." He was born on September 11, 1913.

On September 11, 1983, Bryant's statement took on a whole new meaning for me. While playing a pickup game of football, an ill-fated tackle left me with three dislocated vertebrae in my neck. Rendering me a quadriplegic, I was told I'd never walk again and might be paralyzed from my neck down. My family was advised to place me in a nursing home because I would be too much of a burden for them.

Unable to play sports, I began to read more. I came across Helen Keller's life story and her words struck me: "The only thing worse than being blind is having sight, but no vision."

Despite her disabilities, she persevered through the challenges of life and received a degree from college. Helen Keller inspired me to look hard at myself and the vision ahead of me.

I was blessed with eyesight, academic abilities, and a nagging belief that *something* had called me. Lou Holtz, who coached football at several major universities, once said, "I've never known anybody to achieve anything without overcoming adversity." I figured God must really have a big plan for me because I've had a lot of adversities to overcome.

Confined to a wheelchair at the age of nineteen, I was overwhelmed with the challenges of life. After years of depression, years of thinking about what I had lost, I started concentrating on what I had and could give in life. I now believe there was a purpose to my injury. I don't understand everything, but understand everything, but I sense the big picture. Before being born, God instilled in me the desire never to quit, the determination to fight, the positive attitude to look toward another day, and the ability to succeed in life. Slowly a revelation has become apparent – My life's purpose is to be a positive role model to all I meet. My vision is to help others survive through life's disasters.

Not letting my disability, my personal challenge in life, define me as a person by overcoming adversities and conquering difficulties has made me a stronger individual. Being a successful educator and coach, now a motivational speaker, it is clear that people with disabilities are not limited by their challenges.

Always an athlete at heart, encouraged by admired coaches such as Coach Bryant. His philosophy is burnt in my DNA,

"It's not the will to win that matters." He said, "Everyone has that. It's the will to prepare to win that matters." In May 2011, receiving a doctorate degree in education from Tennessee State University, will not only prepare me for opportunities to help people with disabilities, but will also provide a higher platform to inspire more people.

Finally, brothers and sisters, rejoice! Strive for full restoration, encourage one another, be of one mind, live in peace. And the God of love and peace will be with you.
2 Corinthians 13:11

Chapter One
The Family that Perseveres

Nothing in this world can take the place of persistence. Talent will not; nothing is more common than unsuccessful people with talent. Genius will not; unrewarded genius is almost a proverb. Education will not; the world is full of educated derelicts. Persistence and determination alone are omnipotent. The slogan "press on" has solved and always will solve the problems of the human race.

Calvin Coolidge

I FIRST REMEMBER LEARNING what the words persistence, perseverance, determination, desire, and hard work really meant at eight years old. Not by looking up the words in the dictionary, but by watching six members of my family demonstrate the meaning of the terms. These two men and four women were not only successful in their careers but also in life. My grandfather Jimmy, better known as Pappy, and my father George... worked hard their whole lives to provide for their families and set good examples, being men with strong character. Their lives were short lived because of the hard work they accomplished, providing for their loved ones.

The four women who influenced me were my great-great grandmother, Delia Halter; my great grandmother, Glen Short; my grandmother, Rebecca; and my mother, Kate. These women taught me how to love, care, help others in need, and never give up under any circumstances in life.

All six of these heroes were responsible for developing three young impressionable boys: my older brother, Tim (nicknamed Bear), my younger brother, Andy, and me, the middle child, into the men we became.

My great-great grandmother, Delia Halter, died a year before I was born, but I heard stories about what a hard worker she was. She helped labor the farm back in the late 1880's and 1890's. When times were hard, her children had to push the plow, leaving just ninety pound Granny to be the mule to pull the plow. She is the earliest example found to show how hard working and determined my blood lines go. She made sure that her family would survive even if she had to be the mule.

My great grandmother, Glen Short, got married at the age of fifteen. Her husband left her and their three children, leaving Glen to keep the rest of the family together and make sure they survived. Glen had a job at the phone company in Portland for thirty-five years. She started out working on the switchboard, saying, "Number, please." My mother couldn't wait for the weekends because she would help Glen on the switchboard and sometimes have fun listening in on others' conversations. When the dial tone came into service, Glen worked in a little office where the people of Portland could pay their bills. In time, Glen was promoted to a supervisor.

When the phone company started mailing bills to their customers, Glen started working with her son-in-law in the dry cleaners. He would pick up clothes on Tuesday for cleaning, and Thursday he delivered the clothes to the owners. Glen would use an old wringer washer to clean the clothes and starch them. She then hung the clothes on a line to dry, and the next day she ironed them. She laundered until retirement. Glen died in 1988, just short of her ninety-fifth birthday.

My grandmother, Rebecca Short Dorris, was Glen Short's daughter. She was born in 1915, and we called her Nanny. Nanny played basketball for Portland High School. After high school she was employed by a doctor in Portland until she married my grandfather, Jimmy. She then worked with him at the dry cleaners until she had two children. She was a stay-at-home mom, raising the children and being a wife until the age of fifty-two. Then she decided to go to nursing school and became a nurse. She worked for the hospital for the next fifteen or so years. Nanny died in 2001 just short of her eighty-seventh birthday. The women in my blood line are great examples of determined women who never gave up.

My grandfather, Pappy, was born in 1909 to John C. Dorris, forty-five, and Gertrude Smith Dorris, thirty. The couple had eight children with Pappy being the fourth child. In the tenth grade, my grandfather quit school to go to work so he could help raise his younger siblings. He moved to Indiana to work in a factory and sent part of his income home to help provide for the family.

In 1935, Pappy moved back to Tennessee to start his own dry cleaning business. Three years later he married my grandmother. After World War II, he and two of his brothers became partners. They owned two laundry businesses and sold out in the early seventies. Pappy would come to our house early in the morning in the summer, when school was out. He was growing a garden in the backyard. When I finally got up out of bed, Pappy was already working the garden – tilling, pulling weeds, spraying pesticide to keep the insects away from the plants or placing stakes to support the tomatoes, running lines for the bean plants to grow on, and building mounds for the watermelons. We had rows of corn, beans, peppers, potatoes, tomatoes, watermelons, cantaloupes, and eggplants. When it was time to pick the garden, Mom would can most of the food so we would have some for the winter months. Even in my younger age, I learned to do my part in the garden to earn my food. In 1976, when I was twelve, Pappy had a massive heart attack and stroke. He had worked the garden about half way through the season when he got sick, my mom, my brothers and I finished the season. That was the last garden we planted. Pappy died in 1983, after seven years of being in a nursing home. He was a Lions Club member in its founding year of 1937 and was active in the production of the club's annual Minstrel

Show. While in the nursing home, he received recognition as a lifetime member to the Lions Club.

My dad, George, was my stepfather. No. He was my father, maybe not biologically, but he was the father who taught me about life. He was the one who busted my butt when needed, and he was the one that loved me when I needed it the most. Dad moved to Tennessee from Philadelphia in the sixties. His mother and father were divorced, and he lived with his mother until the age of fifteen. She got mad at him and kicked him out of the house. Dad and his father weren't on good terms either. Dad lived in his car at night, tried to go to school during the day, and worked in a garage after school so he could buy food and whatnots to survive. He quit school at the age of sixteen and became a mechanic full time. When he turned eighteen, he joined the military. When Mom and George met, he was a mechanic for the school system working on buses. They got married in 1970, when I was six years old.

A few years later, I asked Dad about a huge scar on his left leg. At the age of twelve while riding a bicycle he got hit by a bus. The kickstand went through his leg. He showed me a scar on his lower back from the incident as well. The doctors told Dad that he wouldn't be able to walk normally the rest of his life. He was bedridden for a year from his injuries and after extensive, sometimes grueling physical therapy, the wounds healed, and he was able to walk without a limp. Dad's determination to work hard and persevere through the physical and emotional pain resulted in his overcoming the predicted limitations.

Sometimes Dad taught me lessons in life by just standing back and letting me learn by experience. I was able to mature in life while he instilled morals and responsibilities. At the age of twelve, I didn't make the all-star team in Little League. My dad didn't say anything. He put his arm around me to show his love and support for me. That was all I needed.

With my sixteenth birthday approaching, getting a driver's license was the only thing on my mind. My father didn't think the car I had been practicing with would pass inspection. On the morning of my birthday, Dad got up early with me to practice driving his truck.

After about an hour of practice, he asked if I could pass the test. Responding with a resounding, "Yes," we went home to get my birth certificate and money to pay for the test. Turning into our driveway, I hit our fence that surrounded the front yard. When we got out, there was a huge dent on the side of the truck. I just knew getting my driver's license that day was not going to be an option.

My father looked at me and asked if I could still pass the test, this time, with a little less confidence, I said, "Yes." To my surprise, he let me get my driver's license. On the way home, after passing my driver's test, my father told me to take the same route home where I hit the fence. He showed me how to get into the driveway without causing any further damage to his truck. Dad taught me that day that sometimes you have to get past the little picture – the dent in the truck – and look at the bigger picture of what's important (which to a sixteen year old boy was my driver's license).

One More Play

My mother, Kate, is the strongest person I know, not physically strong, but emotionally, spiritually, and character strong. Taking the letters MOTHER, I can describe her to a tee.

Managed to be the jack of all trades. She could help work on cars, build an additional room to the house. She was my personal catcher, doctor, and nurse.

Opened her home to all. She was mother not to just her own children but mother to other children in the neighborhood. She would feed us, correct us, discipline us, provide financial support as well as emotional support. She would be proud of all of us, even though we might have disappointed her.

The nerves of steel. Mom could handle any situation that came to her. She raised her three sons and the neighborhood children after my father died when I was sixteen years old. She came to the hospital with an amazing calm and positive attitude when she found out that I had broken my neck and would be paralyzed the rest of my life. Even after I had attempted suicide, she was there to assure me that things would be all right and she loved me.

Heart bigger than the world. My mom gave twenty dollars a month to a friend of hers, but she did this anonymously. Even when this friend of hers died, she had no idea that my mother was sending her this money. Mom and this friend had a mutual friend who would address the card so her other friend wouldn't recognize my mom's handwriting. One day, this friend of my mother's got mad at my mother and told the mutual friend how mad she was. Somehow, this funding came up in conversation, and my mother's friend said she knew my mother wouldn't do anything like this. Mom still sent the twenty dollars to her until her death.

Eyes in the back of her head. There were times I knew I had gotten away with a particular event, but later on it came back to me from my mother. She questioned my motives and the event. I don't know how she knew or how she found out, but it seemed that there was no way of getting away with my mischievous ways.

Released her love on all occasions. My mother is full of love and is known by numerous people as "Mom." She loves being helpful, being constructive in life, being "hands-on" raising her children, being with her pets, cooking for her family, and being a surrogate grandmother to several families.

My mother is in her seventies and provides life lessons, love, attention, and support to all that are around her. She gives me the courage and strength that I need to continue in life and to become a positive role model for others around me. She teaches me to be strong but understanding, to provide strength and flexibility to others that need it, and to provide open arms as well as an open house to the ones that may need it.

> *Perseverance must finish its work so that you may be mature and complete, not lacking anything.*
>
> *James 1:4*

Chapter Two
INVINCIBLE

*"Your success and happiness lies in you.
Resolve to keep happy, and your joy and you shall
form an invincible host against difficulties."*

Helen Keller

As I lay in bed, I recalled my earlier life, hitting home runs to win the game... about my girlfriend... about pitching a no-hitter... about my girlfriend... about riding around at midnight with some friends... that song on the radio is on again, "King of Pain" by the Police... about cheating on my girlfriend... about my father dying when I was sixteen... and about the time getting kicked out of the game for covering up home plate with dirt because of being mad at the umpire. Memories flooded my mind. I thought a lot about the good times and the bad times. My future wasn't going to be what I had planned, but a future handed to me by someone else. We are all accountable for our actions, and we must either suffer from the consequences of our actions, or rejoice from the decisions that we make. But sometimes we have to suffer or rejoice from the consequences of someone else's actions.

There in the hospital, in the darkness, Anne Murray's song, "A Little Good News Today," came on the radio. The radio has been on twenty-four hours a day. At night time when I couldn't sleep, I listen to music, and reminisce about my life. Did I mention thinking about my girlfriend?

My mind wandered, remembering a lesson learned at thirteen years old. I had gotten into a fight with a sixteen year old from the neighborhood. We were friends, but for some reason we got into a fight that day. We were outside arguing, when my father came to see what the problem was. He sat on the front porch and watched me get the tar beaten out of me.

David had me down and was beating my head like a bongo. After about a minute of hitting my head, David let me up. As soon as he let me up, I hit him in the jaw. This routine played out two more times. Finally, I promised not to hit him, so he let me up. This time I kept my promise by keeping my hands to myself.

After David left, my father was proud of me because I didn't give up. He gave me some advice. He said, "Boy, there is no need to get your butt kicked more than once. One butt kicking is enough when learning a lesson." He continued, "If it takes more than one butt kicking, then someone is not learning from their personal experience. They will always live in pain, regret, and sorrow while worrying why their life is as it is and wishing their life was different." Great advice, but when I was younger, I still needed more than one correction before finally learning a lesson. One big lesson learned was in high school while playing baseball.

As a sophomore in high school, I received the nickname "Grave Digger" from a baseball game. We were playing in Cookeville Tennessee, in the fourth inning, my temper flared at the home plate umpire. As the pitcher, thinking he was making me work too hard for a call, I informed my teammates, I wasn't taking anymore crappy calls from the ump. The team knew my temper and the coach had only heard about my anger but had never witnessed it. That night was his night. At the top of the fifth inning, I walked a batter and was trying to hold him close to first base, by trying to pick him off. The umpire called a balk, allowing the runner to advance to the next base. This pushed me over the edge. Walking toward home plate, tossing the ball up in the air, I could hear the players in the dugout telling the coach that he'd better get out there. After hearing that about three times, I approached the umpire telling him I wasn't going to waste my arm on him anymore. He didn't like being embarrassed as I covered home plate with dirt and placed the ball on it.

"Twenty-three, you're out of the game!" He yelled.

I responded, "That's the best call you made the whole night."

My coach, of course, wasn't pleased with my actions. I was suspended for four games not allowed to dress out, or even sit with the team in the dugout. To stay on the team, part of the coach's conditions was to work extra at practices and support the team from outside the playing field. Then, the coach left it up to the team to vote if they wanted me to be part of the team. Thankfully, they voted me back on the team. For the rest of the season, I was known as "Grave Digger."

During my senior year, we went to Cookeville for another game. I started the game in the outfield. Hitting a solo homerun in the first inning and a two out seventh inning grand slam to put the game in extra innings, the coach decided to put me in to pitch.

After the first two batters reached base with walks, I looked hard at the home plate umpire. Sure enough, it was my old friend from two years earlier behind the plate. My blood began to boil. My catcher called time out and came out to the mound to relay some advice. He told me the umpire wanted me to calm down. I told him to ask the ump why? Was he afraid I would cover up home plate and embarrass him again? We lost the game that night and I learned a lesson. Make a good *first* impression when meeting someone, because you never know when you may meet them a second time.

I graduated from Gallatin High School in 1983. I was the kind of student who put forth just enough effort to stay eligible to participate in sports. I maintained a strong C average... okay; maybe it was a *weak C average*! But I was proud to be able to keep that kind of grade, even though most of my teachers constantly said that I needed to apply myself. Saying, I was much smarter than my grades reflected. My parents definitely told me I wasn't applying myself in my education. I knew that playing baseball had nothing to do with English, social studies, history, typing, and other classes in school. Baseball was my dream, my aspiration, my desire in life. I focused my attention and efforts into playing baseball throughout my high school years. The old saying, "If I only knew then what I know now" is definitely true; as we get older and more mature, we understand this more clearly. If I had been a better student, it would have made things easier when getting older such as finishing college sooner.

I was fortunate to have received Most Valuable Player, All-District, and All-County first teams my junior and senior years. Over the summer, to keep in shape, I played baseball on a college team. This would get me some experience at the college level before entering school in the fall. About halfway through the summer, the coach from Cumberland College, now Cumberland University, in nearby Lebanon offered me an opportunity to play on his team, but he didn't offer a scholarship. I learned this coach rarely offered scholarships to incoming freshmen because he wanted them to prove to him they could play at that level. I originally accepted his deal to be on the team, but later another coach offered me a scholarship. I accepted the second school's offer so I wouldn't have to pay for school. I received a baseball scholarship to Martin Methodist College located in Pulaski, about two hours from where I grew up. I was to start playing there in the fall of 1983.

There were three reasons for deciding to go to college: 1) to play baseball with hopes of getting drafted professionally, 2) to meet girls, and 3) to party. That wasn't necessarily the order of priorities. The order depended on what day it was and what time of day it was as well. If there was no baseball game, I was at college for the girls and parties. If there was baseball that day, then the priority of going to college was baseball. With no intention of graduating, I would do enough work to stay eligible in college so to play baseball. Later, I heard some people from Gallatin were taking bets on when and why I would be back home (whether being kicked out, or failed out of college).

With hopes of getting drafted by the pros, my life was unfolding as planned. Confident I would be the next Mark McGwire, Barry Bonds, and/or Nolan Ryan of my time, I could help my family. They sacrificed so much for me to be able to play baseball. They would travel to watch me play. We would eat late dinners after ballgames and get home late at night. Getting drafted would be my way of paying my family back by purchasing a home for my mother, buying cars for my brothers, and my grandmother – well, what do you give a woman who seemed to have everything? Not knowing what to get her, but I was going to do something.

There was no doubt; my family members were my biggest and most supportive fans. I remember one night my mother, grandmother, and Edna, my mom's friend, drove to Nashville to get me to my first of two games that night. They stayed and watched the first three or four innings of my game and left to go back to Gallatin, so Mom could finish watching the last few innings of my younger brother Andy's baseball game. Then, all of them drove back to Nashville to finish watching my second game. I don't know how many mothers would have done all of that driving and supporting like mine did that night, but I'm glad she did.

I played baseball for two weeks in college. Remembering one practice, there was one player trying to walk on the team. It was his turn to hit, and about that time, the coach got mad at the pitchers because they were not throwing batting practice pitches so the batters could practice hitting. The coach told the pitchers, "This is called batting practice, not strikeout practice." So he took the mound.

The first batter was the player trying to walk on the team. Needless to say, he didn't do very well against the coach. When he finished hitting, he came to me disappointed, saying, "If I can't hit the coach, there's no way he will remember me and keep me on the team."

I told him, "Coach understands that people have bad days."

It was my turn to hit, and I drove the ball all over the park, putting about five balls over the fence. The player trying to walk on came to me and was excited about how well I hit. Playing it down, as if I had had a bad day like him, not wanting him to feel bad, but I knew I had made a name for myself with the coach.

Doing well in sports helped me grow up strong and confident. I had the attitude that I could do whatever I wanted to do, and nothing could get in my way to prevent me from accomplishing my objectives. My attitude was that if something did happen to me, I would get past it because of my strength and determination. I knew that I had this gift of playing baseball, without realizing at that time that God had given me this gift. Thinking the reasons for my success in baseball was because of the enjoyment of playing the game, wanting to improve my play, the desire to play, and love of the game. I was invincible! The only way of preventing me from pursuing my dream would be when I decided to give up playing. My mission in life was to become a professional baseball player, make a lot of money, while gaining the fame and prestige that an outstanding athlete could receive. My special gift was going to take care of my family, while traveling around making a name for myself.

Sometimes our plans don't go the way we hope. Often we have to change our plans or our destiny changes because something goes differently with our lives. There were some signs that life as I'd planned was going to change. Two weeks before I went to college I went four-wheeling with some friends, and tried to stand on top of the roll bar. We hit a bump or hole, and I went flying over the jeep hitting my left arm across the top of the windshield sustaining a major gash. As I was cleaning my arm at home, my mother came in and helped. She told me, "If you don't straighten up and stop doing some of the risky things you're doing, I will be taking care of you the rest of your life, or you will be in a nursing home."

"Mom, you worry too much." I replied. This was two weeks before my destiny, my baseball career changed for the rest of my life due to someone else's irresponsible action.

After one week of college, I went home for the Labor Day weekend and was in the neighborhood playing softball with friends and family. My brother Andy got mad at me and tried to attack me by swinging his fist, trying to start a fight. He was twelve at the time, and I was nineteen. He didn't have the strength that I had, being older and an athlete. He came rushing toward me, and I grabbed him. While he was stopped, I told him, "The only way you would be able to beat me up would be if I were in a wheelchair or lying in bed and couldn't defend myself." After looking back, this was the second sign that was given to me to stop taking life for granted. Remember, my mother said she would be taking care of me the rest of my life if I didn't stop doing the things I was doing.

Two days before my first college baseball game, I met a girl, and was telling her that one day there would be too much pressure put on me, and something serious was going to happen to me. I was sixteen when my father died and became the man of the family. We were an average family, making it month by month financially. But when the roof leaked, and it did, I had to be the roofer. When the water pipes burst, and they did, I had to become the plumber. When the automobiles broke down, and they did, I was the mechanic. While still in high school, I had to keep my grades up, keep the house up, do other chores, and keep playing baseball. There were a lot of responsibilities on me. The new girl told me, "You will need to lean on other people for help."

My response was, "There are too many people depending on me." I couldn't let any of them down.

In the fall, I got to play one college game. I remember going one for two at the plate with a single, a walk, a strikeout, a stolen base, and scored a run. This was going to be a great year.

I was on the road toward what I had been working on since the age of eight. To say the least, I was on top of the world. This day was the beginning of good things. So I thought.

Mother came to me wanting to take me home for the rest of the weekend and then bring me back to college on Sunday. I declined going home and again expressed how invincible I was. I told her the way things were going nothing was going to stop me. In retrospect, this was like the remark about the Titanic. It was said that God himself couldn't sink this ship. We know what happened, don't we? God didn't have to sink the ship; the iceberg did it for him. I rode back to the college with the rest of the team.

Sunday, the final day of my college baseball career, I was playing football with other college students and friends. We were playing tackle, but we were not using pads or helmets. After playing for about two hours, I noticed one guy hit another person high in the neck and head area. I yelled to him, "The way you're playing, you're going to break someone's neck!"

About five plays later, I told my team I was through playing. My leg and toe were hurting, I was getting hungry and needed to get some things together for classes in the morning. My teammates said they needed someone to run the ball. So, I decided to come back for *one more play.* Just one more play.

The football was handed off to me. I saw the hole open up, and scored a touchdown, untouched. Laying the ball down and turning around, I saw from the corner of my eye, something diving or coming toward me. The play was over. I had already

One More Play

put the ball on the ground from scoring a touchdown, but for some reason this person kept playing. Then, I heard a pop.

How hard a hit, I don't remember, but I do remember hearing a loud pop. On the ground, I heard someone yelling that he tackled me. From the hit and the loud pop, I thought my right clavicle, collarbone, was broken. I tried to get up, and nothing followed. Lifting my head off the ground, I tried a second time. My head was the only thing moving, not my arms, not my legs. I couldn't move or feel from my neck down. Something was seriously wrong, then the realization hit me: I was paralyzed from a broken neck.

I started to think back over the signals that were given to me in the past two weeks. If nothing had ever happened to me, then the two weeks prior to my accident would have meant nothing. But when you can't move, all kinds of things fly through your mind. I started thinking about my mother telling me she would be taking care of me if I didn't settle down, how I told my younger brother he couldn't beat me up unless I was in a nursing home or in a wheelchair, how I was talking to that student about having too much pressure put on me and something serious was going to happen. After the baseball game, I remembered saying nothing could stop me, and just minutes ago telling that guy the way he was playing – he was going to break someone's neck. It was all coming into place like a jigsaw puzzle. All the signs meshed together, and now I was paralyzed.

I started thinking about J.T. whom meeting when I was twelve while visiting my grandfather in a nursing home. J.T. was in his early thirties and paralyzed from his neck down from an automobile accident. On the field I started thinking, "I'm nineteen; can't move from my neck down, and will never play baseball again." Not looking forward to going to a nursing home at the age of nineteen for the rest of my life, I started crying.

You intended to harm me, but God intended it for good to accomplish what is now being done, the saving of many lives.
Genesis 50:20

Chapter Three
What Am I To Do With My Life?

*And when man faces destiny, destiny
ends and man comes into his own.*

Andre Malraux

THE DOCTORS WERE waiting for me when I arrived at St. Thomas Hospital in Nashville. People were all over the place around me. They were questioning me, x-raying me, testing me, and, of course, trying to counsel me. They called my family to let them know that I was in an accident, but they didn't tell them what had happened except that I got hurt playing football.

A few months later, my mom told me what my grandmother said about that night. My grandmother used to be a nurse, and she told mom to hope and pray it wasn't a broken neck or a spinal cord injury.

A doctor was doing a pin prick test to understand the level of injury I had sustained. I couldn't feel the differences between a sharp or dull touch in my affected area, but I could tell movement and pressure. I could tell if the doctor moved my toe up or down and which toe he was moving. With my eyes closed, I could tell which arm he was moving and in which direction. Distinguishing the difference between sharp or dull was impossible until he got to my shoulder. It was there I could feel sharpness.

Finally getting a chance to ask the doctor, "How bad was it?"

He responded with, "Bad enough you'll never walk again and possibly not move from your neck down."

"That's pretty bad, isn't it?" I remembered saying. He just stood there nodding his head. I found out that my fourth, fifth, and sixth vertebrae were dislocated.

I continued replaying the last two weeks in my head. If I had just recognized the signs, I would be walking and playing baseball. I would be in my bed getting ready for class the next morning. Instead I was lying on the Stryker frame, a frame used for people with spinal cord injuries. It is used because of the limited movement by the patient, if any movement at all, so that nurses and doctors can place the patient in different positions to increase blood circulation and prevent bed sores.

A situation I will never forget was the insertion of screws for my new head-gear. The screws were to attach tongs, so ten pounds of weight could hang from the end of a rope. This was to provide resistance, hoping my neck would stretch out so the vertebrae would go back in place.

Before they put the screws in my head, the doctor told me they were not going to put me to sleep and it would hurt like hell. "I can't fight you. Do what you need to do." I replied. The doctor drilled holes in my head. Pain seared through my brain... the noise of bones breaking... the sound of the drill... pain, *unrelenting pain* was unfathomable. Time seemed to stand still as I felt caught in this web of never ending trauma. The screws were in place, but I doubted ever being the same again.

Later that night, my mother called my high school baseball coach to let him know I was paralyzed and in the hospital. He asked what happened. Mom responded, "Playing football."

He came to the hospital that night. Telling him what the doctor had said about not walking again and maybe not moving from my neck down. He responded with, "You have never listened to anyone else before, so why do you want to start listening now?"

While on a Stryker frame, I would lie on my back for two hours. Then the nurses would strap another part of the Stryker frame on my front and turn me and the bed. They turned me like they were flipping pancakes in a pan. Then they would take off the part of the Stryker frame from my back, and I would lie there on my stomach for one hour. So every one or two hours, I was being turned, 24/7, for the next two weeks.

When awake, the doctors and nurses would ask me questions to see if I had any brain damage. Questions like – What's your name? How old are you? Who is the president of the United States? Do you know where you are? Do you know what happened to you? One day they asked me what day it was. I had no clue, but I remembered getting hurt on Sunday, September, 11, 1983. Yes, I had my 9/11 years before our great nation suffered from 9/11. They then told me it was Thursday, September 15. I had lost four days of my life.

I remembered waking up a few times, but not realizing I was in critical care. Once I woke up and heard someone yelling in pain. I asked the nurse what was this guy's problem. She told me he had stomach problems. I went back to sleep, woke up later, and didn't hear screaming this time. I asked, "What happened to the man with the stomach problem? Did he get some Pepto-Bismol?" The nurse informed me he wasn't here anymore. I remembered responding; "Now some people can get some sleep around here."

Months later, I found out he died. Being young, it never occurred to me, for some people a hospital stay might end in death. The reality of this place, what could happen, became glaringly obvious. While avoiding pain was the goal of the day, medication became a good friend. Sleep formed an escape and depression came creeping in...

Family members were well aware of the new "normal", and did what they could to offset my negative decline. I mentioned that my grandmother, Nanny, had been a nurse. One day while I was facing the floor, on the Stryker frame, Nanny came to visit with a ladder. I didn't know what she was doing other than moving up and down on the ladder. She said she had a surprise for me, something I needed. So for the next hour, lying on my stomach, Nanny worked at a frantic pace.

When it was time for me to be turned over, the nurses came in for the *unveiling* of "Nanny's Creation." All eyes were on me, as I was turned over, revealing the surprise of my life! The ceiling was filled with gorgeous pictures from a Victoria's Secret catalog – for my personal enjoyment. I wasn't surprised that she did this because she had a great sense of humor, and we as a family, have always played jokes on each other. Thank you, Nanny, *for the gift that kept on giving,* every time I was "face up."

One day I was talking to a therapist and asked about my injury. She told me that it only takes five to seven pounds of pressure to break a neck. Then she went on to tell me that with my weight, the other person's weight, the force of the hit, the gravity pulling us to the ground and the impact on the ground, there was probably 800 to 1,000 pounds of pressure that landed on my head and neck. If I hadn't been an athlete, I probably would have died.

Knowing I had a spinal cord injury, couldn't move from my neck down, and had limited sensory feeling. But nothing could have prepared me for my new label: "A quadriplegic." This so traumatized me, I became sullen, finding it hard to speak for days.

At this point of desperation, a ray of sunshine entered my life. Her name was Vicki. She was a Middle Tennessee State University student, who worked at St. Thomas Hospital part-time. Vicki was not only compassionate, intelligent, funny and naïve, but also had this bubbly, upbeat positive attitude. She was very beautiful, not only on the outside, but had beauty within her heart. The first time meeting Vicki she was quiet, not talking unless I started the conversation. I must have made a grand first impression: strapped to the Stryker frame. She would come in, do her job and leave, not wanting to wake me up or bother me.

One morning crying, thinking about everything I had lost, tears slowly fell down my cheeks. About that time Vicki came in, took a Kleenex and wiped my tears away. She informed me that things were not as bad as they seemed. Good things would be coming. Suggesting that I needed to be strong, she would help me through this dark time in my life. Not being able to do something as simple as clean my face from crying, was an embarrassment. I then told myself it was okay for a man to cry, but only if he could wipe away his own tears. That day I tried not to cry while others could see me – I cried myself to sleep behind closed doors.

Vicki didn't start work until eight o'clock in the morning, but she would show up at 7:30 to visit me before anyone else had a chance. She would wake me up with her pleasant, lovable personality that made me feel like a man. Don't tell anyone, but she would give me that good morning kiss that would get me started for the day. As it was time for her to get started for work, she would hold my hand and tell me that there was a purpose for my life. She said God wouldn't let my life waste away lying in bed... this paralyzing situation would accomplish God's glory in my life. I wasn't a Christian then, but I enjoyed holding her hand and losing myself in her eyes. Vicki would hurry to get her other jobs completed, to feed me my breakfast and shave me. She was wild about Old Spice, sometimes putting so much on me that I got sick. But never once complained about the attention she gave me, bathing and dressing me. Her time with me seemed magical. I would come back from morning physical therapy, and not long after, Vicki would come in to make sure I worked my hardest and did my best at therapy. She reminded me I needed to use the same determination, desire, and fight from baseball, to beat this situation. Then, as always, she would feed me my lunch and hold my hand. I realized that Vicki was the angel that God put into my life to keep me from being depressed. I needed her to help me accept my future.

After two weeks in the hospital on a Stryker frame, I needed surgery to align my spine. The weights hanging from the tongs didn't help my vertebrae to go back in place, so the doctors wanted to operate on my neck to correct the dislocated vertebrae. The morning of the surgery was Vicki's day off, but she came anyway to comfort me. A nurse came in the room earlier than scheduled to take me to surgery. My mother and Nanny hadn't gotten there yet. As the nurse was taking me to prepare for surgery, she told Vicki, "The other wives are in the waiting area."

"Yes honey, you can wait with the other wives." I replied with a smile on my face. Vickie smiled and gave me a kiss on the cheek.

The surgeons wrapped wire around the dislocated bones and cut my hip open and took strips of bone from my pelvis to place on each side of my vertebrae to stabilize them. The screws were removed from my skull, and there were no more weights hanging.

Shortly after surgery, I had limited movement in my arms. Other tests showed that my spinal cord was still intact. That meant there was some hope about recovering from my injury. If the cord had been completely severed, there would be no possible hope of returning any movement from the point of injury down. I could move my arms at the shoulders and biceps, but there was no movement in my fingers, wrists and triceps. With the excitement that some movement was coming back and with months of physical therapy, I would be back to normal, or at least be able to walk, I still faced the reality that baseball was over.

For the next three months, I was on a rollercoaster ride because of the physical and emotional ups and downs. The doctors and nurses would come in and tell me to try and move my big toe on my foot. I needed to concentrate on little movements first before trying to move larger muscles. Every now and again, while lying in bed, I would try to move the big toes of my feet, which seemed hard if not impossible, due to the lack of sensation. I couldn't see my toes while on my back, so I had to rely on what feeling I still had. After a week or ten days, one night I was trying to move my big toe on my right foot and I felt it move. I took a deep breath and concentrated on my right toe again. I focused on moving it, and again I felt it move. Because I was on my back, I couldn't see the movement, but I knew with all my heart I moved my right big toe – I felt it move. I called for the nurse to come into witness my movement and celebrate the miracle of the first step, or wiggle, on my come back tour to a walking normal life. The nurse came in, and I told her to watch my big toe, that I had moved earlier. She stood there and watched. I took a deep breath and concentrated on moving my big toe. When I felt it move, I exhaled with the excitement of defeating paralysis, starting with my big toe. The nurse looked at me and told me that my toe didn't move. I told her she must be looking at the wrong toe and that she needed to watch my right toe – my right big toe. I took in more air and focused on moving my right toe. Again, the nurse told me that my toe didn't move – the right toe didn't move. The emotional ride that night went from excitement of beating paralysis to feeling totally defeated and helpless. Becoming overwhelmed, I was depressed and went to sleep.

Even though I gained movement in my arms, they were very weak. I needed help eating, getting dressed, performing my personal business, turning in bed, changing the television, turning the radio, holding the phone so I could talk with people. Well, let's just say it: I couldn't do anything with my weak arms. One night I had a bright idea. I wanted to reach and touch the floor. I have no idea why I wanted to touch the floor except that I could say I did it. I got my right arm between the bed rails and started reaching for the floor, when a nurse came in the room. She pushed me back in the bed and scolded me about how I could fall out of the bed and get hurt. She said, "What would you do if you broke your hip."

I replied, "If I broke my hip, I would tell people I broke my hip trying to touch the floor. It wasn't because the nurse did it helping me in or out of bed. It was because I did it trying to do something without help from anyone else."

The nurse stayed at my door watching me the rest of the night. I didn't get to touch the floor. Yet, another night of feeling like a failure continued.

Weekdays were better than the weekends. I got attached to the weekday nurses more than the weekend nurses. Maybe because I stayed in bed on the weekends, while on weekdays the nurses got me up for therapy twice a day. The weekends were very boring.

One day, while the nurse was taking my vital signs, I had a fever. They took my temperature later, and I still had a fever. A nurse came in about 4:30 in the morning to take my blood so they could determine the cause of the fever. The next morning a nurse came in again and drew blood because I was still running a fever. The third day in a row, they drew blood because they still hadn't determined what was causing the fever.

A few days went by, and apparently my temperature went down and no one came to draw blood. Where they had drawn blood, my arm looked as if I had the measles. There were about nine red dots on my arm. Then, one day, while a nurse was collecting my vital signs, it was apparent the fever was back. She ordered my blood drawn again. When the other nurse came to get my blood, I refused to let them do it. They had drawn blood for three days in a row and didn't find the source of my fever. So what made them think getting blood this time would produce the magic number needed?

The nurse threatened to tell my doctor that I was refusing to cooperate with the procedure. I told her to tell the doctor they were not going to take my blood. The nurse then made the mistake of telling me if I refused, there was nothing they could do. I looked at her with a big smile on my face, telling her they could not get my blood.

The next day, my doctor came in and explained they really needed my blood. He promised this would be the last time. I agreed to it. Later on, we found the cause of my fever was a urinary tract infection, which is typical for spinal cord injuries. I received antibiotics to correct the problem.

One nurse who became a great friend was Randy. He had a positive attitude, inner strength, and a beautiful heart as well. Randy gave both of us nicknames. I was "Bubba one," and he was "Bubba two." It wasn't too confusing and it was fun. Randy would come in full of confidence that overflowed. Being the only male nurse on the floor at that time, he allowed me to talk to him man-to-man. Since we were "Bubbas," he wouldn't break my confidentiality. And yes, I opened up to him about how I felt about Vicki.

Randy told me he had a little girl with a disability, and he knew how I felt. He knew all the hard work that was needed to overcome this adversity. Having a little girl with a disability might have been God's way of preparing Randy to take care of me.

My physical therapist, Debbie, was an awesome little firecracker. She was able to use her techniques and leverage to maneuver me like a sack of flour. Always positive, she encouraged me to be open-minded, unafraid to explore what my body and mind could still do. At first, she would come to my room to stretch my limbs and prepare me for therapy. Since I had been lying on my back for weeks after surgery, my flow of blood had been moving in a vertical position. Debbie warned me that my blood pressure might drop when I first sat up. She wanted me to sit on the side of the bed for a few minutes and get used to being up again... telling her if I got dizzy or felt sick, so she could lay me down on the bed.

One day I was sitting on the side of the bed, and Debbie asked me how I was doing. I replied, "Okay." Apparently I wasn't okay. Before I knew it, I woke up hearing a train coming. I had passed out, not giving her time to react to me. But guess what? I touched the floor that day and didn't break my hip or anything else!

When starting physical therapy, I was wrapped up as if they were wrapping a Christmas package. Wearing a neck brace, thigh high hose on my legs to help with blood circulation, elbow pads to help prevent bed burns and a binder around my waist to keep me from passing out. All I needed was a bow on my head, to be placed under a Christmas tree. I looked forward to therapy, not only to work and get better, but also for companionship. I was anxious to meet new people, talk with different individuals and most of all, getting out of my room.

There was one patient named Fred who quickly touched me. He walked into my room and said, "James?"

I said, "Yes, sir."

"I'm Fred," he said. Vicki and the other nurses had told me about him and his real estate business.

"Fred! I've heard a lot about you." I replied.

Fred said, "I'm not here to talk about me. I'm here to see if what I've heard about you is true." He was looking at the room full of encouraging cards and my grandmother's decorations.

For the next three days, Fred and I talked about my future. He was an older gentleman who had kidney stones, yet, was a very positive person to be around. Having been successful in Real Estate, he encouraged me to look for the silver lining in the dark clouds.

After a week of hospital stay, Fred was dismissed to go home. He stopped by my room on his way out and said, "James, it was my pleasure to have met you. If I can do anything to help you, please, don't hesitate to call."

About an hour later, Vicki came into the room with a letter from Fred. As she was reading it to me, I noticed she was crying. Here is Fred's letter:

Town Properties, Inc.

Fred R. Webber
PRESIDENT

Oct 10 26 1983

Dear James,
    As I have laid in my bed just down the hall from you this past week at St. Thomas Hospital, at night, when the halls were quiet, I have wondered, like you, "why"? Not why a kidney stone sidelined me for a few days, but why you happened to fall as you did, and be sidelined indefinitely. Its one thing for a 59 year old man who has had a rich and full life, to be incapacitated for a few weeks, but quite a different thing for a 19 year old boy, in the prime of his manhood, to be so severely tested. James I have never been tested, as you will be — physically — but we all, at some point or another, in our lives, are faced with adversity. My test, more mental than physical, came during World War II, and if you will let me share some very private things about those times — some for the very first time, then perhaps in some small way I can inspire in you the added desire to more quickly overcome some of your adversities.

    In 1943 I was 19 — a free spirit — like you — the world was mine with a fence around it. I played all day and

Town Properties, Inc.

Fred R. Webber
PRESIDENT

and sometimes all night. A war which I knew little about was going on in Europe. But that, I didn't think, was my world. That was someone else's world — some else's problems. Suddenly the crescendo of world conflict swept me up in its clutches and in a few brief months I found myself side by side, with others like me, struggling against the outgoing tide at Omaha Beachead on the coast of France — praying to God that he let me live long enough to reach the beach and find cover from those who were just as interested in stopping me. James, my friends were sinking from sight, all around me, some so close that when I tried to hold on to them, I had not the strength to save a fellow man. Boys like you are now James, with fuzzy faces, rebuilt trucks, girl friends, moms & dads, brothers and sisters, high hopes and many other things. These young men, the cream of American youth,

Town Properties, Inc.

Fred R. Webber
PRESIDENT

going back to their maker, in the cold icy waters of the Atlantic. This was it — there wouldn't be another chance. No loving mothers eyes to look down on them and say a million prayers — no brothers arms to support them — when they could not support themselves. I made it ashore James — one of the lucky ones. However, in that space of a few hours I lived a lifetime. I know now what I gained, but I only thought then of what I had lost, I never thought it would be the same again. I feared my mind would be infested forever with terror, pain, and lonesomeness. It took a while James — it took everything I could give not to quit and say "This isn't what I had counted on" "I've been delt a dirty blow" "I want to go home" or "I have no future". I guess I may have thought some of those things, but to dwell on that was folly.

One More Play

Town Properties, Inc.

Fred R. Webber
PRESIDENT

Like you I lived, and with the help of others — doctors, counselors, therapists, family and friends, I was able to overcome severe mental shock, and put my life back together. I pray you will be able to do the same — and you know something — I have no doubts but what you will.

Good luck James, and don't hesitate to call me if you ever need me.

God Bless You

Fred

Mr. Fred and I maintained contact for years. In 2009, I called to see how he was doing and his wife told me Fred had passed away. His letter comforted and inspired me so much that I read his letter years later to my students, always on October 10, the date he wrote the letter to me.

For I know the plans I have for you," declares the LORD, "plans to prosper you and not to harm you, plans to give you hope and a future.

Jeremiah 29:11

Chapter Four
Spain, I Can't Speak Spanish

"I've never known anybody to achieve anything without overcoming adversity."

Coach Lou Holtz

AFTER ABOUT SIX weeks in the hospital, I knew my neck vertebrae bones were healed because, when in seventh grade, my left leg was broken while playing flag football and it took six weeks for it to heal. It was in the morning, and dew was on the ground. The football was thrown to me, running down the sideline to score the touchdown; I tried to stop to put a move on a player in front of me. When putting my left leg out to come to a stop, my foot slid out from underneath me, and my weight fell on top of my leg. After getting up, I couldn't put weight on my left leg. My mother took me to the hospital for x-rays. A week later, it was confirmed there was a hairline fracture in my tibia. I should have known by this fracture football wasn't for me. Like Dad said, "If it takes more than one time to get your butt kicked…" After six weeks, the bone had healed. So naturally after six weeks in the hospital, my neck had to be healed.

One morning going to physical therapy, I told the nurses that it had been six weeks, the bone had healed, and I didn't want to wear my neck brace any longer. Also, no more wearing elbow pads, white leg hose, or a binder! I wanted to go to physical therapy looking like any other person with a disability, not one that looked like a mummy. They agreed to lose the elbow pads, binder, and hose, but they wanted to wait for a doctor's order about the neck brace. If nothing else, I have learned to be persistent in my life, and kept telling them that broken bones heal after six weeks. Reluctantly, they gave in to me. As we were going to physical therapy, my neck muscles were so weak that my head was bobbing up and down, sideways, and I laid my chin on my chest because my neck muscles were straining and hurting trying to hold up my head. Maybe this wasn't a good idea.

When arriving at physical therapy, they noticed I wasn't wearing any of my protective gear and wouldn't touch me during physical therapy without a doctor's prescription. So they took me back to my room, and the therapists put all the items back on me, including and especially the neck brace. By then, I had missed the first round of physical therapy that morning. But in the afternoon, all geared up and protected correctly so I would be ready for a hard day of physical therapy.

The next day, I told the nurses the same thing about not wearing any of the protective wear. Since they didn't put them on me the day before, they didn't ask any questions and didn't put them on me again. So off to physical therapy I went. When getting there, the physical therapists couldn't believe I was there again without my neck brace and other protective material. But I was extremely persuasive and assured them the doctors gave me permission to have therapy without my gear. After about a week, everyone was sure that I had permission, and we were working hard twice a day. There was no concern about working me out and being afraid of hurting me.

On October 31, I made a muscle in my right leg move on my own, not a muscle spasm, but me. I just knew in no time I would be back to normal. The nurses called Vicki for me. I asked them not to tell her about the movement in my leg because I wanted to hear her excitement after she received the news. They called Vicki and told her to call me. She was as excited and started crying from being full of joy. Vicki even came up that night to witness me gaining some strength by showing her the muscle movement in my leg. As a reward she stayed there for about an hour holding my hand and kissing me. She was making me feel as normal as anyone could be. I didn't feel like a handicapped gimp that needed help. Her touch and concern made me feel like a whole man again. Vicki looked a lot different after work hours than during work. Her hair was down, out of a ponytail, and she had put on makeup. She had that sweet smile and a twinkle in her eyes. She was what the doctor ordered. When she left that night, I could hardly wait for the next morning, when she would wake me up. I was falling in love.

In a week or two, both legs had a little movement, but very little strength to do anything. I was weaker than a baby. I even made the comment that babies could move all their body parts, but they couldn't communicate if and when they were having problems. On the other hand, I could communicate when something was wrong, but couldn't do anything about it. However, the thought of regaining use of my body was utterly exciting.

The therapist helped me in bed after physical therapy one morning, and one of the doctors came to visit about that time. The nurse wanted me to demonstrate my leg movements. Showing off – I extended my legs and flexed them as well. Then one of the therapists started telling the doctor how much I had improved by not only moving my extremities, but also by not wearing the binder, elbow pads, thigh hoses, or neck brace. Quietly in that moment, I surprised everyone in the room with the comment, "and I had no permission to remove the items." The nurses and therapist were mad at me. The doctor agreed that I could stop wearing everything but the neck brace. While in bed, I could leave the neck brace off. The jig was up.

One day the occupational therapists had a surprise for me. They wanted me to learn how to feed myself again. I couldn't hold a fork because my hands and fingers were too weak, so they strapped these devices, called a cuff, around my hands so I could hold on to my eating utensil. They even had a device that would hold my arm up in a sling. I was adamant about not going to eat that way. It wasn't the normal way someone should eat. But I wasn't normal anymore; just looking at these devices made me feel disabled and useless. They argued about needing to learn how to feed myself so I could gain more independence. I still continued saying I wasn't going to feed myself that way. Then they asked the wrong question: "If you don't learn how to feed yourself, then how are you going to eat?"

I replied, "My mother will bring Bojangles, and she will feed me." Bojangles is a fried chicken restaurant that was strategically placed on the corner next to the hospital.

They just looked at me and said, "When we see your mother, we will talk to her about not feeding you so you will learn how to feed yourself."

About that time, my mother walked in with Bojangles in her hands, and looking at the occupational therapists I told them they could leave now, it was time for my lunch.

My grandmother, Nanny, was in the room with me, all alone. We started talking about my situation. I told her I would rather gain my legs and walk than have arms that were working. I said to her walking was more important than knowing how to feed myself. She said for me to listen to myself, and then she educated me, if I was walking and couldn't use my arms, then how would I use the bathroom? If you are walking, and the door in the room is closed, how can you get out if you can't use your hands to open and hold the door? She told me to be careful what I wish for – I just might get it. She gave me a lot to think about that night.

After three months at St. Thomas Hospital, I was discharged to spend six weeks at Spain Rehabilitation Center in Alabama. It was considered one of the best rehabs in the South.

The morning I was discharged, the nurses gave me a sendoff. Randy, "Bubba two," Vicki, and a few others helped me into the ambulance and wished me continuing improvements and success. After three months of being a family, it was time to leave. Vicki was the last one to say, "Good-bye," and she gave me a card. She told me not to read it until I was on the road to Birmingham. One of the paramedics read Vicki's card to me. Here is Vicki's letter:

One More Play

Dearest James,
 I wanted to give you this card early, so that I could say what I wanted. #1. We had *lots* of *great* times together these past 9 weeks & 2 days — & I loved, truly loved every one of them. #2. I want *you* to concentrate on James & *no* one else, so that you'll get better faster. #3. Work real hard for both of us. #4. Keep in touch with me during your stay in Alabama. #5. Make new friends, but me cute BAMA girls. HA! #6. Try to diet while you're down there — because I'm going to try & I'm going to win our bet. #7. Come back up to St. Thomas & visit us when you return from Alabama (& I had better be the 1st one you see)!!
 James, you never know what will take place in the future (or these next 6 weeks). But one thing I know is that there will NEVER EVER be another James Perdue in my life! (Especially Tim).

I also want you to know that all of my players & my family's & friend's prayers are going with you. James, my God richly bless you, as he has me by letting me meet you & take care of you. Thinking of you at Thanksgiving James, Is a very "special" way a very, very you are Of bringing us together part of my "SPECIAL" For a little while today, life. But then it seems
all through the year
We're never far apart,
For many pleasant memories
Always keep you close in heart.

"Happy Thanksgiving"

Vick

P.S. I can't wait to hear from you. Take care of yourself, & behave!!

As we went to Alabama, I thought of the great times with Vicki and all of the other people that took care of me.

When arriving at Spain, I noticed two things: first, there seemed to be people who were in worse shape than me. They were lying in bed, had on halos, and nurses seemed to be doing everything for them. There wasn't much interaction among the patients. I was feeling guilty because of the movement in my arms and legs, and because of being stronger.

Second, others there were better than me. One man, with his halo, would stand up to pull up his pants. Another man, when he stood up, would walk around the room with nurses' assistance, at least once an hour. I started feeling bad that I had not improved as much as them. Thinking, I gained movement in my arms and legs before arriving at Spain, by discharge time I would be walking out of the building. After all, this was one of the best rehabilitation centers in the South.

After a month, while learning to feed myself and rolling my wheelchair, there was no improvement in my legs. This rehab focused on my return, not on what might return. They were trained to help people become independent after the injury instead of finding a cure for paralysis. I didn't understand. I thought they would help me regain strength in all my body, not just in my arms. It was frustrating.

After six weeks, it was time to be discharged to go home. The doctor told my family to place me in a nursing home because I would be too much of a burden for them. My family and I didn't ask questions about how to do certain things... manipulating my body to achieve daily physical chores... or how to use assistive devices to be successful. Being new to this 'being paralyzed' and they were professionals who turned me loose, with far less than adequate training. Wasn't it their job to teach me how to make it in this world?

> *In everything I did, I showed you that by*
> *this kind of hard work we must help the weak,*
> *remembering the words the Lord Jesus himself said:*
> *"It is more blessed to give than to receive."*
> *Acts 20:35*

Chapter Five

Readjusting to Home Life

"Remember today, for it is the beginning of always. Today marks the start of a brave new future filled with all your dreams can hold. Think truly to the future and make those dreams come true."

Author Unknown

J<small>UST A FEW</small> weeks before Christmas, I returned home from Alabama. On the drive back from Birmingham, my oldest brother Bear was telling me about Michael Jackson's new video *Thriller*. We pulled in the driveway about 2:00 A.M. Mom, Bear, and I had training from Spain in how to provide therapy stretching, transferring, personal hygiene, and other important things – but how do I get out of a vehicle? Bear was trying to get me out of the car and into a wheelchair when I passed out. While trying to pick me up, my neck brace cut off my air supply. When waking up, I noticed Bear kicking the fence. After calming down, he got me in the wheelchair and into the house. This was going to be a hard adjustment, not for just me but for all of us.

A few friends from the neighborhood came over to visit. The television was on MTV so I could catch *Thriller* for the first time. After about two hours of catching up with my family and friends, we all needed to go to bed. Mom and Bear transferred me to the bed, and then Michael Jackson was coming on. They got me up and out of bed to *Thriller* and then back to bed.

Sleeping about fifteen to eighteen hours a day, I stayed in denial. Being home with no hospital or doctors was the reality I had been avoiding and dreading – my condition was permanent. On Christmas day, when it was time to open our presents, my mom and brothers opened mine for me. I tried to stay positive and excited, but this was boring. My mother later said that was a sad day for her, watching someone else opening my presents.

In January of 1984, I began the year with the goal of entering college. However, going back was an excuse to get out of the house and meet other people. I didn't return to Martin Methodist, but chose to attend Volunteer State Community College. Vol State is a two-year college in Gallatin that I had avoided earlier because of wanting to leave my hometown. I signed up for one class, a coaching class, because of all the preparation needed to get ready for class with someone dressing me, bathing me, and driving me to class. All this would take a lot of effort. One class at Vol State would be plenty with all the special attention I needed. Bear drove me to school, got me out of the car, and pushed me to class two times a week. After class was over, he would return to take me home.

In the afternoons, we started our own physical therapy program... doing leg and arm strengthening exercises for about forty-five minutes, with wrist and ankle weights following for another forty-five minutes. During my arm exercises, someone would put wrist weights on and perform with me. We would take a break until time for bed. Mom would bathe me in bed, and my brothers would stretch my legs and help me do leg exercises. As my legs got stronger, we added more exercises for my legs. We started standing me up in front of the kitchen sink. My mother would be on my left side, and one of my brothers would be on the right side. There was a belt around my waist, and my arms would be on their shoulders. They would grab the belt and count to three – up I would go! At first, I could stand no more than fifteen seconds at a time, but later I was standing three to five minutes in one session. Listening to the music of Def Leppard helped me gauge my time standing.

Later, my first steps took place on homemade parallel bars. The bar length was about seven feet long. Taking a few steps, someone placed my wheelchair behind me so to sit down when getting tired. Finally, when getting stronger, I could turn around and walk back to my wheelchair and sit down. Eventually, I was walking seven laps, back and forth, on the parallel bars before needing a break. I felt like I had run a mile. Walking several times a day was one of my workouts for the day.

After about seventeen months of our therapy program, I was able to stand for about ten minutes and walk about fifty feet inside of the parallel bars. Becoming bored and mad that my recovery was taking longer than anticipated, Bear pushed me in my wheelchair down the road one evening around midnight to visit Bobby. He lived with his grandparents, and his grandmother used a walker to get around. I asked about borrowing it. When we got home, Bear helped me stand up, and I took two steps with the walker before falling to the floor. Bear turned me over to see if I was hurt, but he saw the excitement in my face because of the lame attempt to walk, even if it was just two steps. Since it was about one o'clock in the morning, it was time for bed, but couldn't sleep because of the thrill of walking outside of the parallel bars. After about a year and five months, I had taken two steps.

The next morning I wanted to stand using the walker again, but couldn't get up. I kept trying with still no progress. Frustration mounted, because just the night before I did stand. All I was doing was wearing myself out and getting mad. While leaning on the walker, I observed Bear stand up from the couch. I asked him to sit down and stand up again. For the next ten minutes, I studied his actions, trying to figure out the problem, using him as a model. Sometimes he would move at a normal speed, and other times he stood slowly.

Realizing the problem, I was trying to stand in a straight line – my body was rigid and leaning backwards. My body and mind had forgotten how to stand. I noticed Bear would bend his upper body over his legs. He was getting his weight over his center of gravity and then using his arm to push up and contracting his leg muscles at the same time. He continued leaning and moving forward until he was standing. After simulating Bear, attempting ten or twelve times, I mastered standing from my wheelchair. This skill gave me tons of confidence for trying other homemade experimental therapy programs. This was my main way of transferring to the bed, the toilet, the shower, in the car, and anywhere else needed. Finally, standing for ten minutes at a time felt good. I knew walking after climbing this mountain was possible.

Now motivated more than ever, remembering doctors saying I would never walk again and possibly never move from my neck down. Making a liar out of the doctors for at least ten minutes was a positive step. By using more arm and ankle weights I could build more strength. The stronger I got, the cockier I got as well. I was working out for a purpose – walking. I could see the light at the end of the tunnel, and I knew it wasn't a train coming. This was awesome.

It doesn't take much humiliation to bring someone back down to Earth. My brothers helped me on a weight bench one evening so I could build more strength. Even though my biceps, deltoids, and forearms were getting stronger, my triceps were still paralyzed, but I was thinking about getting them stronger. Before my injury, I could bench press over 200 pounds. Being centered under the bar, and knew bench pressing that much weight was out of the question, so I had them put half of what I used to do – one hundred pounds.

Well, not only was lifting one hundred pounds out of the question, but I also couldn't get my hands up to the bar. My triceps were dead. Dumb me still didn't give up – yet. Stubborn me wanted to press the bar with no extra weights on it. My brothers used ace bandages to tie my hands to the bar. Bear stood by to spot me in case I couldn't lift the bar off. Yea, right, in case I couldn't get the bar off me. Bear lifted the bar, I gave the word to let go and bam. The bar hit my chest and knocked the wind out of me. Bear got the bar off and I caught my breath, but did I learn my lesson? No. I wanted to try again, and my brothers still supported and encouraged me, but the same thing happened. This time I got off the bench and never tried that again.

When I wasn't working out, I attended classes at Vol State. In the fall of 1984, taking four classes, twelve hours of course work. Even though attending classes, I sat there listening, but didn't take notes. Even if I could write, reading my handwriting was next to impossible. I did my projects, homework, and any other activity to help balance all the quizzes and tests failed. Needing to ask for help would benefit me, but my pride wouldn't allow me to ask – the semester wasn't a stellar one. My mentality was the same as it was in high school – just stay eligible: eligible for what I don't know. I just didn't want to flunk out of school, but not want to be there either. I was barely able to maintain a C average.

I signed up for classes in January of 1985, for the express purpose of getting away from my mother and brothers. Education had nothing to do with this decision. I needed to get out of the house. It seemed reasonable to maintain a C average and family life would be healthier with distance between us.

One More Play

At this point, depressed more than ever, I had gone through depression, but this feeling was different. I was sleeping more, eating more, and snapping at the ones who were trying to help me the most. My mouth spewed constant anger that had apparently been brewing inside me. One time, after verbally assaulting my closest target, my brother Bear, he took a gallon of Gatorade and poured the whole thing on my head!

Previously, Andy got mad at me. Again, it was something I said. I don't remember what it was, but I deserved what he did as well. Andy picked up the front end of my wheelchair and turned me over. I didn't have the strength in my arms and legs like before the injury, so sometimes, "my mouth wrote checks that my butt couldn't cash." I said things out of frustration causing my family to be hurt.

Going to the baseball park to watch games was my therapy. I could still enjoy the game, allowing me to exercise my mind even if I couldn't play.

One night I decided to stay home and let the rest of the family go to the park. So my mother thought she would stay home as well. Firmly informed her, I wanted to be by myself, and was tired of seeing her and my brothers. While watching a movie, an ambulance went by the house to the hospital. About seven minutes later, Mom came rushing in to the house because the ambulance went by the park and she thought something had happened to me. Wouldn't you know it? The first time I'm home alone and something still seemed to go wrong. Time at home wasn't pretty with all the arguing, stress, and my personal daily pity party. I knew I had to leave so everyone could have a break.

In May of 1985, it was my decision to withdraw from Vol State. I wasn't putting forth my best effort, going for the wrong reasons, and could meet people at the store without wasting money on education. Knowing life wouldn't improve by staying home, I made a phone call to the Tennessee Rehabilitation Center (TRC). TRC is a vocational training facility that trains people with disabilities so they can receive employment.

After speaking to a vocational rehabilitation counselor and explaining what was going on, and my needs... I was put on a waiting list. The center would let me know when there was an opening.

About three months later during September, I received a phone call about an opening in physical and occupational therapy. It meant a move to Smyrna, Tennessee and a much needed break for my family. In that facility, I met other people with spinal cord injuries and learned how to do more things for myself in hopes of becoming more independent. We learned from a therapist, as well as each other. We shared advice about what we thought would help each other from our own personal experiences.

When trying to learn to dress myself while lying in bed, it was too hard and required more energy than was needed. There was a rope that was in the shape of a ladder attached at the foot of the bed. By grabbing a rung and pulling myself up, I could get my pants started on my feet and legs. Then roll to my left and to my right side while trying to pull up my pants. After catching my breath, putting on my shoes, finally, transferring to my wheelchair, I needed a nap. There had to be an easier way.

When first arriving at TRC, I used a power wheelchair. There is a difference between a power chair and an electric chair. At that time, I didn't know that but learned fast. I met a man and told him I liked his electric chair. That was a mistake. He assured me that he wasn't a criminal. Criminals go to the electric chair whereas people with disabilities use a power chair. Then, if that wasn't bad enough, he put his arms out and started vibrating like he was being electrocuted. I never confused the term "electric chair" with "power chair" after that.

One day during physical therapy, I went to the parallel bars and stood up. People couldn't believe I was standing. One of the therapists said, "You messed in your nest." After that, they gave me a manual wheelchair to get around. Maneuvering around like the others, my arms were getting tired and sore, but I was getting stronger and also having a good workout.

I discovered a way for me to get dressed and not wear myself out. While sitting in my wheelchair, I began dressing myself. I would sit in the chair and open my pants or shorts. Then pull them over my feet and up to my mid thighs. When it was time to pull my pants up, I stood up and finished dressing. After a few months of therapy, I went home, continued using a manual chair but determined to leave it behind permanently.

In the summer of 1986, I was MAD. Mad at the world. Mad at myself. Mad at the paralysis that held my body hostage. So to tackle the anger within, I set a goal of pushing myself a mile in my wheelchair. I hadn't pushed a mile before, but I was in the mood to do something that would help me get stronger. I used to run a mile before my injury, and I had a place marked off. So I knew when I pushed a half of mile and wheeled the same distance back it would equal a mile. Bear pushed me down our gravel driveway and got me on the road to start my one-mile journey. I wasn't pushing to set any time record or going for a leisurely stroll. This was a test to see if it was good therapy.

The first half mile was no problem since it was mostly downhill. But then the dilemma became the angled slope of the roads. Roads are built for water runoff, but the road engineers never figured on a large man, in a rolling vehicle – such as a wheelchair. It was a fight to keep my "rolling chariot" out of the ditch! I got to the end of the half mile, and it was time to go back. I didn't lose much muscle strength on the first half so I thought going back would be okay. It would be hard, but I didn't think it would be too bad. Then I turned around and saw how much uphill work there would be. I couldn't just sit there because it was getting dark, so I headed toward my biggest challenge of the day: the half mile return of the "Lone Wheeled Stranger!"

As I continued going back home, I could only go about twenty feet before my arms would get tired and sore. I would stop pushing and take a break for a few minutes. This happened numerous times before I finished the mile. About a third of the way back, I noticed a car was following me. Honestly, it was getting dark, and he was making sure I got home safely by flashing his head lights to warn other cars, but I didn't take it that way. Being mad at the world, now I was getting mad at this jerk for following me.

About half way home, a police car came up; knowing the officer, I yelled, "There is a person in the car who wants to rob me or something. He keeps following me." The officer assured me I wasn't being robbed, there were several calls about someone in a wheelchair on the road, and it was getting dark. I explained that I was getting some exercise.

So, the friendly officer who was there to protect and serve me, followed until I got home. He even had his blue lights flashing! This was an apparent "get away" of a different kind. No doubt, the neighbors had plenty to talk about that night! (This was 1986, a decade before that infamous white bronco chase in California.) I was going about half a mile an hour, and the blue lights were behind me making every stop I was making and moving forward when I was moving forward. During one stop, the officer got out and we discussed finding a place to push so it would be safe for me. *Really?* I'm no Albert Einstein, but after this excursion... even I was not anxious to do this again. After about an hour, I got home, and the officer was on his way to protect and serve other people in the city. After that adventure, I started pushing on Vol State's campus for the exercise and for the safety.

In the summer of 1986, I participated in wheelchair sports in Birmingham, Alabama. This was an area contest, and the winners moved on to other competitions. This would be the first and only time I ever competed in wheelchair events. It was amazing to watch these athletes compete, but it wasn't for me. The first thing people had to do was take a physical that determined the level of strength and ability of each wheelchair competitor. People with similar strengths and abilities would compete against each other.

I watched wheelchairs cruise around the track at speeds that seemed to be thirty miles per hour. There were people lifting weights, pushing on the track by themselves, and, as a team, participating in club throw, shot put, javelin, discus, swimming, ping pong, tennis and other sports, just like regular people. I competed in the club throw, shot put, and swimming events.

In the shot put, each person threw this heavy metal ball three times, and the farthest distance was kept while the other two throws were cancelled. The shot put was heavy, especially when you don't have much strength in your arms and hands. The ball sits in your hand, and you pitch it as far as you can. It didn't go far at all from me.

The club throw was different. The club was designed like the shape of a bowling pin but smaller. On this day, someone forgot to bring the club, so we used a glass coke bottle. Yes, a glass coke bottle, the opening end of the bottle was between my first two fingers, and I threw it over my head for distances. I was worried more about hitting my head with the bottle or that the glass would break by hitting a rock, but neither happened. Both sports were interesting, but it didn't do anything for me and my competitive spirit.

The two swimming events were held indoors. I was watching other people swim, and this activity was getting my adrenalin running. It was time for my first swim event, and watching my competitors practice, I was feeling sorry for them. They looked weak and uncoordinated from their limitations, and I didn't think it would be fair for me to embarrass them, but I had to do what I had to do.

The only swimming we could do was the back stroke. We would drown if we tried to swim face down because we couldn't turn our heads to get our mouths out of the water to take a breath. I climbed out of my wheelchair and sat on the floor. Then I made my way to the final destination – the water. We were in the water with our arms on the side of the pool, and the horn sounded for us to start the race. I pushed off the wall and started my back stroke and was still thinking this wasn't going to be pretty. And I was right! This wasn't going to be pretty at all.

The sporting competitive nature, that I hadn't felt in nearly three years kicked in. The sound of the crowd made my adrenalin flow throughout my partially paralyzed muscles. In the water, I felt light and agile. I was moving like no one's business. Thinking about how I hit the winning homerun in a game, pitched a no hitter, and the awards that I earned. It all happened because of my hard work, determination, and the competitive drive that was in me. This was great. I had found a sport in which I could learn to love and participate.

I looked to my left and to my right, and there was nobody in the other lanes. I was beating them so bad that they were nowhere in sight – what a great feeling. About halfway through the race, my arms were burning and hurting. I had hit the wall, not the pool wall, but my energy was depleted. I wasn't going anywhere. The crowd was still cheering, but the harder I tried to swim the less I was moving. I started thinking that I could grab the ropes, the ropes that divide the swimming lanes, and catch my breath and finish the race. As I reached for the rope, about four able-bodied people came to my rescue. They brought me to the side of the pool to make sure I was fine and helped me out of the pool and into my wheelchair.

The reason I didn't see anyone else to my left or right was that they had all finished the race. I was the only one in the pool, and I was dragged out of the pool as if I was a huge catfish on the bottom of a lake. It was so embarrassing that everyone saw me needing help and not finishing the race. I pushed my wheelchair out of the pool area and into the dressing locker room.

The recreation director from TRC who had organized the trip, friends, and other athletes came to comfort me. I was in tears and didn't want to hear what they had to say. But there was one recurring phrase that came up – they were telling me that I didn't have to swim in the next event. Swimming again was not an option. I wasn't going to swim and they couldn't use reverse psychology to talk me into it. I didn't care what anyone thought of me for quitting. I wasn't going to be publicly embarrassed like that again.

After about fifteen minutes of feeling sorry for myself, I heard the announcement that the next swimming race was about to begin. They made the announcement calling for the swimmers in the event by name. After hearing my name, I continued saying I wasn't going out there. Hearing my name for the second time, I didn't budge. Then I heard, "Last call for James Perdue, or he will be disqualified." I've never forfeited, been disqualified, or quit a game before, and the competitive spirit in me wouldn't let me go out like this.

I pushed back to the pool and repeated the effort like before, I entered the water to get ready for the race – or at least – try to finish what I started. This second race could have been a DVD replay of the first contest. My muscles were hurting, burning, and I was going nowhere. This time I knew not to grab for the rope. I kept swimming or at least moving my arms, even though my body was stationary. Then I was hit by an inspiration. Not in my head at first, but in my foot. I could touch the bottom of the pool, so I decided to use the strength in my legs to push off the pool floor. Propelling through the water re-energized me with a determined mission – to finish this race. I was moving three or four feet at a time. There was no stopping me now. I know – you're thinking he cheated. You can look at it that way, but as I see it, I explored my options and used my creativity to finish the race. And by the way, I finished third in the shot put.

In the fall of 1986, I returned to Vol State to continue my education. I took a full load, but again not for the education but to get out of the house. I did enough class work to keep my financial aid available and to keep me from being on academic probation. Studying just wasn't for me, but the opportunity to socialize was what I needed at the time.

In one class, I met a woman who seemed to be a saint. She had adopted over twenty children with disabilities, and she was furthering her education as well. I was talking to her one day about how I missed driving and losing the independence of getting out by myself. I was dependent on someone to drive me to class, the store, the movies, and any place else I needed to go. I told her that I bought a car for $500. It was a 1977 faded orange Chevrolet Cutlass with a half-torn vinyl top. The brand new tires were worth more than the whole car. I figured if something went wrong, whether I had an accident or just couldn't drive due to my injury, I wouldn't be out of a lot of money. I was telling her I needed hand controls on my car so I could learn to drive again.

I tried driving without hand controls, but that ended up not being a smart idea. There are different types of hand controls. These controls were attached to the steering column, brakes, and gas pedal. The hand controls are manipulated by placing the left hand on the lever. When pressure is placed on the lever toward the dash, the brakes are operated. The gas pedal is maneuvered when the lever is pushed down toward the lap.

Since there were no hand controls, Bear would be in the car with me as needed to assist. One afternoon while practicing my driving skills, I thought I could handle driving as if I were "normal" again, so I started using my legs and feet. The practice drive went pretty good. I had my left foot on the brake and my right foot on the gas. My hands were at ten and twelve o'clock. We went up and down the driveway several times, and I told Bear I'm ready for the road. I hadn't driven in over three years and still had limited movement in my arms and legs. We went about five miles away from home. I was driving the speed limit and feeling good about driving. We got home safely and without any major problems. With more practice, I would get better each time.

A few days later, my mother wanted to go to the store, so I offered my car as transportation. I put one foot on the brake and the other on the gas. The rest of the family got in my car, and off to the store we went. I backed out of the driveway and was heading down the street when I noticed the car was acting up. There was a miss in the engine. Since my arms were weak, I knew, if the car stopped running, I wouldn't be able to apply enough pressure to the brakes or enough strength to turn the steering wheel to get off the road to a safe place. So I decided to go back home.

As I turned the car into the driveway, I hit a hole that caused my left foot to fall off the brake, and my right foot had a muscle spasm that caused my foot to extend on the gas. We were flying up the driveway with no brakes. I saw the tree in front of me and swerved to my right to miss the tree, but then I saw my mother's car. I swerved to my left and missed her car; then we were heading for my neighbor's house. As we were gaining speed, I was yelling for Bear to put his foot on the brake. He stopped the car with just a few feet before colliding into the house. I yelled at Bear, "What were you waiting for?"

He replied, "I thought you were trying to show off."

That was my last day driving with my legs. Hand controls cost about $500 and that was money I didn't have. After sharing my adventure, this saint of a woman came to class the next week and gave me the cash to buy my first hand controls. Freedom and independence had come at last. I believe she was more excited seeing me drive onto Vol State's parking lot than I was.

In October of 1988, I then returned to TRC for their bookkeeping program. Individuals there worked at their own pace to assure they are confident about what they learn and are prepared for employment. For example, to get a Bookkeeping I certificate is considered a nine-month program. People work at their own pace, someone might take ten or eleven months to complete the program, while someone else might take eight months. I took the program, was focused, and finished the nine-month course in three months. That's right – three months. Then I decided to go for my Bookkeeping II certificate, which required three additional months. I relaxed some and took my time and completed the program in two months. I graduated with a Bookkeeping II certificate that took me five months to finish instead of one year.

I applied to work with the State of Tennessee and was called for an interview. I didn't get the job. One of the reasons was my fault, because of having an attitude during the interview. Even though cruising through the program at TRC, I was considered under-qualified because of not having 1,500 practice hours on my transcript. With all A's, one B, and graduating, the transcript showed 537 practice hours, two-thirds fewer hours than the state recommended for this position.

My comment, "Even though working hard and quick to prove I know the material, but because of not having 1,500 hours of practice I'm not getting the job." I left the building confused and heartbroken.

One More Play

A month later, I was hired to work at a travel agency as a secretary. Although I didn't do bookkeeping, the owner, Carolyn, taught me how to help people with travel plans. It was a great opportunity to gain employment experience, and Carolyn became a good friend. Grateful she took a chance on me, and giving me hope that there are other people like her out in the world. I was there for about five months when Carolyn decided to retire. Uncertain about what my next move would be, I thought about going back to Vol State.

A professor from Vol State came by the travel agency, and I talked with her about continuing my education. My problem was I didn't want to take the time to find out what was needed to get started. I don't know if I was just being lazy or just unsure if I really wanted to go back to school because I had gone back several times and had not been serious. She took my Social Security number and came back the next day with a year's schedule of courses to take. If doing what was on the list, I could graduate in one year. I couldn't believe she did that for me. Not many people would go to that much effort for another person.

Since she did all that work for me, I'd better try again, so in January 1990, it was off to Vol State. This time I wasn't going to college for baseball, partying, to meet women or even just to meet people. This time wanting to graduate, I start studying. My class load was difficult and heavy. This surge of effort was a turning point for me. I decided to focus on studying, by passing these hard classes, it would indicate the seriousness on getting my education.

Bear gave me this advice, "Take the determination, hard work, and perseverance that you used in baseball, and apply them toward your study." Advice well received.

I signed up for fifteen hours of classes, which included biology with a hard instructor. After our first test, he wrote out test results on the board. The instructor was writing up A's on the test – zero, B's – five, I don't remember how many for the C's, D's and F's.

Well, not being an A person; a B person, I studied hard and hoped for a C. Hoping I didn't receive a D or F. My paper came back with a B. Not only happy, but also this was a sign I was capable of doing college work. Next to me was a student named Mark who got an F on his paper. After class, he asked me about my grade. Informing him I was one of the five people that got a B, acting like I earned these grades all the time. So I asked him what grade he received on his paper.

He surprised me with his response, "I believe that if you believe in the Lord, He will provide."

I said, "Pardon me if I am wrong, but I think the Lord has provided you with these books so you had better start studying."

He asked me, "Where are you going to be in the next few minutes? I'm going to my car and get my Bible so I can save you."

I said, "Save me? I'm the one who got a B; I didn't fail the test." Needless to say, when he left to get his Bible, I left like Elvis leaving the building.

A few days later, Mark caught up with me and wouldn't let me out of his sight. I used to go to church when I was younger, but I didn't read or study the Bible. I used to go, sit, listen and never talk about the lesson. Now I had been in a wheelchair for about two years. I was bitter toward life, and it wasn't that I never knew there was a God, but I found it hard to believe in one.

Mark started in on me about being saved, so I fired back at him. I asked him, "If there is a God, why did this happen to me?"

He tried to explain that God wanted to show he had control over me – that's why this happened to me.

I then replied with, "I was just playing a fun game of football. Why did God do this to me, but he would let these drugs users and drug sellers sell drugs to kids that are nine, ten, eleven years of age? Why did God do this to me, but He will let drug dealers live in million-dollar homes and drive fine cars, so why am I so special?"

He had no answer. I even came back with, "If God wanted my attention, He could have just broken my finger as a warning. I don't want to know your God who inflicts pain. I want to know a loving God, a God that will be there when I fall, a God that will let me know that He loves me when I'm down about how life sucks." Again, he had no response.

I finished the spring semester with one C and the rest were A's and B's. I'd never been committed to studying and learning like this ever before. I remembered studying for my history mid-term exam for four days and got a ninety-four on it. I was talking with another student, and she told me she studied an hour before the test and got a ninety. I took that information as I studied four days to her one hour and I got four extra points – awesome. The preparation was long and difficult, but the rewards felt great.

I took four classes in the summer, having two classes in each of the two five-week sessions. This was my first summer session, and after it was over, I would take summer classes every chance I got. The classes were long during the day, but the instructors had to present the most important information, so I felt that I learned more. I finished with A's and B's. Soon the summer classes would be over, and fall classes would begin.

Four classes were all I needed in the fall to graduate with my Associate Degree. After two semesters of college requirements, my confidence was flying high. I couldn't wait to get started so I could get done. Plans were made to attend another university in middle Tennessee, Middle Tennessee State University in Murfreesboro. Again, finishing with A's and B's. College didn't seem as bad or as hard as people said, as long as I put forth the effort. Realizing instructors are there to help because they want to see people be successful. But I had to make sure to do my part as well.

In November, I received a letter that presented deadlines on getting my cap and gown for graduation and an award ceremony with breakfast the day before graduation. I decided not to participate in graduation but instead have my degree mailed to me. The deadlines went by, and I was satisfied with my decision.

A week before the awards and graduation I was going from one building to another when I met Vol State's president, Dr. Hal Ramer. He congratulated me with my accomplishments and said he would be looking forward to seeing me at graduation. I didn't want to tell the college president that I had no intention of participating in the ceremony or wanting my degree mailed to me, so I told Dr. Ramer that I couldn't be in the graduation ceremonies because I missed the deadline for ordering my cap and gown. He assured me he had connections and he could make it possible to graduate with my peers. I thanked him, and we went on our different ways.

Driving home, I was hoping Dr. Ramer forgot about his connections and I could be back to my plan – degree by mail. While getting my wheelchair out of the car, my mother came to the front door telling me I had a phone call. After getting into my wheelchair, I went into the house. On the phone was someone in charge of the graduation at Vol State who needed my height and weight so my cap and gown could be ordered. My plan was gone, and now participating in the graduation ceremony. You can't win them all.

Mom accompanied me to a breakfast award ceremony held the day before graduation. Individuals were recognized for academics from different departments, community involvement, and other areas. I didn't pay attention because I knew I wouldn't receive an award. My GPA was just average, and I did nothing special at Vol State to have deserved an award.

Toward the end of the ceremony, Dr. Ramer got up to talk, and I thought the program was over. Then he started a speech about a certain person who worked hard, showed perseverance through troubled times, and didn't let adversities stop him from achieving a degree. He described how this person was making a difference in other people's lives. I stopped eating and started listening to him. I leaned over to Mom and said I would like to meet this person. Then, Dr. Ramer announced, "The winner of the Dr. Ramer Award for Overcoming Adversities goes to James Perdue." I looked at Mom and couldn't believe that his speech was about me. Not only did I receive the award, but I also found out this was the highest award given by Vol State. I should have figured that out because it was named after the president, Dr. Ramer.

He told me that people would watch me and that I wouldn't necessarily know who or when. They would want to see how I handled myself and my situation. He said that people would use my courage and perseverance to develop the strength to get through the day. Most of the time, I would never know when someone was watching. He hit the nail on the head with that statement. People came to me and told me they didn't think they could do what I did if they were paralyzed. I just said, "We never know what we can do unless we're in a particular situation."

The next day I graduated. People that I haven't seen in years came to congratulate me for not giving up, especially after my injury. The next step was to continue my education at Middle Tennessee State University.

Your beginnings will seem humble, so prosperous will your future be.

Job 8:7

Chapter Six
I Can't Quit My Education Now

"Only as high as I reach can I grow, only as far as I seek can I go, only as deep as I look can I see, only as much as I dream can I be."

Karen Ravn

JANUARY 1990 ARRIVED, and it was time to move an hour away to Middle Tennessee State University (MTSU), so I could start the next step on my educational journey. Bear and Mom helped me move in and get settled. They hung my clothes, stocked the refrigerator and shelves with food, made my bed, and placed my shower bench in the shower with other personal hygiene products. I said, "Good-bye. I love you" they returned the same responses.

The first day without my family, I met other people in wheelchairs. Each had different stories about how they were paralyzed, but the diagnoses were similar. We all lost our dreams we had wanted as we were growing up and had to start over in our new adjusted lives. I met one man who wanted to fly planes, one who wanted to drive trucks across the country, one who was a drug user, and one who was an unofficial philosopher. I noticed there was another common denominator with the group. They all liked beer. I drank very little because I didn't like the taste and also because when I played baseball, I didn't drink. I was naive about professional athletes. I thought the good, or should I say "the great," athletes didn't drink.

Actually, the first time drinking a beer I was put in jail. It was on my high school graduation night. I was in the car with four other fellow graduates, and we were celebrating. One of our bright grads threw a beer bottle out of the window and, wouldn't you know it, the police were behind us. I was the only one who passed the field sobriety test, but was charged for under-age possession of alcohol. Earlier that night, my mother had reminded me, "If you drink anything, don't drive." Well, I didn't drive. My years of playing jokes caught up with me. When I called mother to bail me out, she hung up the phone because she thought I was playing a joke on her. She finally realized that I wasn't kidding, and she paid my fines. I knew then that drinking wasn't for me.

The next day I registered for four classes at MTSU – twelve hours of higher education. I was excited to be on the way toward finishing my bachelor's degree. When it was time to pay for my classes, a huge surprise hit me like a ton of bricks. I was told that I owed about $1,500.

While at Vol State, I received financial aid in the form of Pell Grants and also vocational rehabilitation money. I continued receiving these funds for my education as long as I was attending college and kept my grades up. Since Vol State is a community college, I didn't have to pay for living on campus. In addition, the amount of money per hour was less than at MTSU, so by the time I finished paying my tuition, there was over $400 left over to pay for books and gas to drive back and forth.

After explaining this to the financial person at MTSU, I still owed $1,500. Thinking I would receive more money in Pell Grants because of going to a four-year university compared to a two-year college, but found out that the financial aid was the same amount no matter where I went. Also, no longer being a vocational rehabilitation client after I graduated from Vol State was a problem. I found out the hard way and in an embarrassing manner that a four-year university was more expensive. That day I called my family, and moved back home. Instead of twelve hours, I signed up as a part-time student and took six hours or two classes.

Driving an hour one way and an hour back twice a week for sixteen weeks for two classes was my only option. The courses were challenging, and it might have been a blessing not getting in as a full-time student. Two classes at a time helped me get my feet wet to adjust to the different teaching styles and to gain more confidence in my studies. I wasn't a scholar before, but I earned two A's that semester. I thought about taking the summer off, but I remembered the summer classes at Vol State, so I took the two additional classes. Now I was driving four times a week for the next ten weeks.

Over the summer, I met with my vocational rehabilitation case manager so I could become a client again. This way I could afford MTSU as a full-time student. I had been dropped from vocational rehabilitation because of a dispute over getting a ramp built at my house. My brother Andy and a friend Bobby built a ramp when I first got home from the hospital, but it was so steep that it took two people, one person pushing and the other pulling, to get me into the house.

Vocational rehabilitation was happy to help by building a better ramp. I got three bids as they requested, but while they were processing my request, I was accepted to the Miami Project in Florida. Miami Project was a research hospital for spinal cord injuries. Since I would be in Miami for three to five months, vocational rehabilitation postponed building the ramp. When I returned four months later, I had to start the process again.

After submitting the three bids a second time, I started TRC's bookkeeping training. After five months of education, I was home. But I didn't accept their reasoning for not building the ramp this time because I came home every weekend and holidays. I wasn't out of state, so I could have used the ramp.

My mother fell down the steep ramp and broke a few ribs. After contacting my senator and explaining the situation, the accessible ramp was built in less than a month. Because of going over their heads, it was later determined I was no longer a

One More Play

client in the vocational rehabilitation program. They have done all they could for me.

After meeting with the vocational counselor in the summer, I became a client again with one condition: if I had any problem with them or services being provided, I was to contact their office first. I agreed. There were no problems, and I believe they provided proper services. Since being a client again, they helped pay for my education as a full-time student. We were all winners this time.

I learned vocation rehabilitation agencies supplied other students with disabilities with their own computers. After contacting my case manager about this situation, a computer was delivered to me two weeks before I graduated. The computer was a year and a half late, but I got my first computer, as a graduation present.

With tuition costs covered, I moved back to MTSU in the fall. My roommate, Ray, was born with cerebral palsy. He was a senior and would be graduating after two semesters. We became pretty good friends. Ray was in love with a student named Beth. If we needed Ray and he wasn't in class, we knew to go to the bookstore, because Beth worked there.

One day while going to the bookstore to find Ray, and, sure enough, he was there. As I was getting closer, Beth was explaining to him why he was in a wheelchair. Being the inquisitive guy, I wanted to know why as well. She was telling Ray that we were in a wheelchair because of our sins. Ray was listening to her, and it looked as if he was accepting her explanation. Beth was telling him because of his sins is the reason he was in a wheelchair. But she didn't show or tell any Bible scriptures to back up her explanation. I couldn't keep quiet.

Asking Beth if what she was saying were true, then why isn't everyone in a wheelchair. Knowing very little about the Bible, but I did know that according to scripture, we all are sinners. I could buy into her explanation if we were all in wheelchairs because of our sins. Asking her the same questions that were asked to Mark, I was just playing a game of football. Why did God do this to me, but let these drug users and dealers sell drugs to young kids? Why would God let drug sellers live in million-dollar houses and drive fine cars? Why was I so special?

Then Beth's explanation became even more interesting. She explained that my sins and Ray's were worse than other people's.

Then Ray asked Beth a brilliant question. I was surprised that Ray would even question Beth because he was so in love. Ray then said he was born this way and he didn't have time to sin, so what happened to put him in a wheelchair.

Then I joined in and asked Beth to please explain that. Again I could understand her early explanation if we were all in wheelchairs, but explain why Ray was born this way.

Beth then continued that Ray was in a wheelchair because he was paying for his parents' sins.

Responding quickly, I couldn't and wouldn't believe in her god. Who would want to know a god who seeks revenge on his people for doing wrong? I looked at Ray and told him he needed to leave her alone because she was a witch.

It was amazing to me that two people, Mark and Beth, church-going people, let me know the reasoning for being in a wheelchair was because of a god who was controlling, inflicts pain and suffering due to my sins. If I were them and didn't have a better church answer than they had, I would keep my mouth shut.

For years I've been trying to find out why this had happened to me. Wondering what the purpose of my life is, I found myself getting depressed, madder, bitter, and questioning if there was a god, why does bad things happen? Around people I would put on a front. I heard on more than one occasion, "If I was in your place, I don't think I could do what you do."

Sitting up straight I explained, "With two choices in life, I can sit back and let other people take care of me or I can get up every day and make the best of life." People believed I had my life and circumstance under control. But by myself, I would wonder, "What am I really going to do with my life?"

> *Have I not commanded you? Be strong and courageous. Do not be afraid; do not be discouraged, for the LORD your God will be with you wherever you go."*
>
> *Joshua 1:9*

Chapter Seven
It's Off to Work I Go

"Anyone can give up, it's the easiest thing in the world to do. But to hold it together when everyone else would understand if you fell apart, that's true strength."

Author Unknown

GRADUATION FROM MIDDLE Tennessee State University in 1993 launched me on my next venture: finding a teaching position. I received my degree in education, and felt I could be an inspiration to younger people by encouraging them not to give up. If I could get out of bed in the mornings and do everything necessary to get ready to teach, they could come to school with a headache and learn. I thought I wouldn't have a problem getting a job.

Pursuing every job opportunity, I applied to thirty-five different counties in the state. At every interview I emphasized overcoming my disability with hard work, perseverance, and determination. Certainly my potential employers would see me as a positive role model for their students. After twelve interviews, as it turned out, no one else felt the same way about my overcoming adversities and being a positive role for the students. Spending my summer filling out applications and going on interviews, no teaching position was offered.

Without a full-time teaching position, I applied for substitute teaching at Gallatin High School. After a school year of subbing, my summer was again filled with applying and filling out more applications to more school systems. Fifty counties in Tennessee, half the counties in the state, now had my application and resume. There were a few months of driving 3,000 miles a month picking up applications and going on interviews. After pursuing fifteen more interviews that summer, still no teaching job was offered.

In the following year, 1994, I continued substituting at Gallatin while driving to Middle Tennessee State University to work on my master's degree. In December, White House High School offered me a teaching position. Excited from the opportunity, finally, a chance to prove I could do the job. I was teaching there half the school year, while driving to Middle Tennessee State University, and coaching a summer baseball team. It was a busy time for me. This was an interim position. At the end of the school year, the position would go back to the original teacher, but now I had experience.

After I finished my Master's Degree in Education in the summer of 1995, I didn't fill out any more applications. After

One More Play

completing eleven interviews with no success, there was one more position line up. This interview was about an hour and a half away. I called them two days before the interview and asked if there were any teaching positions for biology, physical science, or health available. If not, since living an hour and a half a way I wouldn't make the trip. The person who answered the phone assured me that there were plenty of teaching positions still available. Driving the hour and a half for the interview, the superintendent spent fifteen minutes with me and then told me there were no positions open at this time. I said to him, "I called on Monday, and I was told there were plenty of openings."

He responded, "All the positions have been filled since then."

I asked him, "Then why didn't someone call me so I wouldn't have to make the hour-and-a-half drive?" It was getting harder and harder going on interviews and staying positive. It was hard to hear over and over, "No, this position is not for you," or waiting by the telephone that doesn't ring.

Finally, the hard work and perseverance paid off. I had an interview at a middle school in the county. The principal met with me for the longest interview yet – about an hour. After the interview, the principal walked me to the door to let me out. As we were going out of the office, noticing a man in his nice suit with a briefcase in hand, standing in a military stance as I was leaving. I didn't know him, but when seeing him I knew he would get the position I was interviewing for, and once again I would not get a teaching job. That afternoon the principal called me and offered me the position.

The next day at an inservice, and this man from the day before came up to me with a briefcase standing in a military stance. He put his hand out and introduced himself to me as Rick. He was hired at the same school. Rick was teaching sixth grade science, while I was offered a science position in the seventh grade.

In the middle of the school year, I received a letter that stated I was nominated for an award from the mayor's advisory committee office of Davidson County. It was called The Jo Andrews Award. This award was presented to a person with a disability who had overcome adversity. Later finding out, my instructor from TRC nominated me, because of pursuing my desire to become a teacher.

When contacting the office to find out about this prestigious award, they informed me Jo Andrews was instrumental in advocating for the disabled during her time in Nashville. In the eighteen years this award was given, I was the first person nominated who wasn't a resident of Davidson County. Since persevering for three years in search of a teaching opportunity and not stopping until receiving a position, not only nominated for the award, but also the winner. This was the highest award the mayor's advisory committee can bestow upon someone with a disability.

Rick and I became co-coaches of the girls' basketball team. As co-coaches, we trusted each other to make the right decisions; we worked the girls' hard and expected dedication and loyalty to the team. Our first season together wasn't pretty. As coaches, we were limited in basketball knowledge, and finished second to last place that year. Over the next couple of months, we both got videotapes, went to basketball clinics, got advice from other coaches so we wouldn't embarrass ourselves, the school, and our girls basketball team again. We became the middle school version of Pat Summit, the Lady Vols women's basketball coach.

Our conditioning program was second to none. We were proud of the program we developed, even though the girls were a little afraid of it. Part of our plan was to work the girls into the best shape possible before the season started, so we could win our games in the fourth quarter.

Conditioning began after the first full week of school until the first practice. We conditioned for about eight weeks. That way we could work on practicing basketball and getting ready for the games, knowing that the players would be in great shape. We used our practices for basketball to reinforce our conditioning. Before most games, Rick and I would talk strategies to use against the opponents, adjust our strategy during halftime, and after the game discuss what strategies needed improvement on before the next game.

Over the next six years, we finished first or shared co-championships in the regular season. We either finished champions or runner-up champions during the county tournament. We even won the T-N-T State Tournament once. Not every game was perfect, but we believe that we gave our best to all the girls to help them become successful, not only on the basketball court, but also in life as well.

A game that stands out in my mind was a championship game. The opposing team had beaten us twice earlier in the season. The first time they beat us by thirty points, and many people, including the players and coaches, were surprised that we would get beaten this badly by the other team. All summer it was the talk that our team and this certain team would be playing for the championship. So for this team to beat us by thirty points was unexpected by all of us. We practiced harder and smarter so we would be better prepared for them the second round.

The second time we played them, they beat us by one point. We had the last shot of the game with about four seconds left in the game and missed it. We finished runner-up to this team in the regular season, earning the opportunity to play them again in the championship game. Before the game, Coach Rick and I had a big, fired-up speech and motivational talk to get the girls pumped and ready for the contest. I told the girls that one of two things could happen that night. One; we play as hard and as smart as we can and end up on the victory side of the contest, or second; we could let them run all over us and basically be a doormat allowing them to do so. Then pulling a doormat out from behind my back and pitched it on the floor. I told them, "Don't be a doormat for anybody or anything for the rest of your life." The girls walked on top of the doormat proclaiming their championship.

With twelve seconds left in the game, we were down by one point. Coach Rick and I had one of our girls tell the referee that we were fouling one of their players before the ball was put into play so no time would come off the clock. This foul would put the other team on the free-throw line for a one and one. The player we fouled had missed several free throws during the game. With twelve seconds left in the game, the player missed the front end of the one and one, and we got the rebound and brought the ball up. We called a timeout with about nine seconds left in the game.

We took the ball out at half court and had our best player get the ball and attack the basket for a layup. As she went up, the other team fouled her, putting her at the free-throw line shooting two shots. With about five seconds left on the clock, our player made both free throws, giving us a one-point lead. The other team quickly got the ball in, attacked the basket, and got the ball in the paint. One of our players blocked the shot to end and win the game. We were tournament champions again with only two losses for the season and eventually went on to win the T-N-T state championship.

Rick and I coached together for seven years and dominated our county in middle school basketball. Rick became my best friend, and I looked up to him because of his Christian beliefs and his outstanding morals.

We taught our players more than just basketball. We taught them to help other people whenever possible. One way we did this was through a student named Jennifer. At the end of her sixth-grade year, she got off the school bus and started to have seizures. The seizures continued through the summer, and she was getting tested to see what was causing her seizures.

In her eighth-grade year, she was told to come to school and stay in a wheelchair all day long because when her seizures started she would fall to the ground and bang her head. By staying in a wheelchair, if she started having a seizure she would already be sitting down. Tests showed that the nerves in her brain were overlapping both sides of the brain causing her seizures. The doctors recommended that she have half her brain removed to help prevent her seizures. At that time, she would be the oldest person, fourteen years old, to have this type of surgery. Younger patients' seizures stopped, and with half a brain Jennifer could retrain neuropaths in her brain. She could learn to do everything the whole brain used to do. The doctors told Jennifer that by removing half her brain, they felt confident that her seizures would stop, but because of her age, they didn't know if she would recover enough to walk and talk again.

Coach Rick and I decided to make Jennifer an honorary Lady Buc. We gave her a uniform and made her part of the team. She got into the games for free like all the other players; she could come into the locker room for pregame, halftime, post game, and hear all the strategies and corrections needed for the game. We actually had a pep rally before the first game of the season, and announced to the whole school student body that Jennifer was an honorary Lady Buc. The team signed a basketball and presented her with a uniform. Jennifer got to see her name on the wall with the other basketball girls' names. One of our players' parents knew someone who had coached with Pat Summitt, and the Lady Vols sent a signed basketball as well. We had great news coverage so this would be a very important event for Jennifer.

Why did we do this for Jennifer at that time? We needed to do it before she had her surgery so she could comprehend and be excited about what was going on because she may not know or understand it after the surgery. By presenting her as an honorary Lady Buc before surgery, she could feel good about herself and be excited about this special event in her life.

Jennifer left to have her surgery in New York, and the news stations from Nashville did several reports on Jennifer and her progress. When she got home, our season was over. We won the county championship, and since Jennifer was part of our team, we got her a trophy and championship T-shirt.

After the surgery, Jennifer had to learn to walk and talk again, but she had no more seizures. She has been a role model for all people who know her because she had the strength, confidence, and courage to face her struggles and not give up. For our basketball girls, they learned to give back and think of others with physical challenges greater than their own.

After seven years, Rick decided to leave the school for another. I missed Rick and coaching wasn't the same, but I became the head coach and was able to make him proud. I was fortunate and blessed enough that God sent me athletes who would listen, be hard workers, and were dedicated to the sport. These weren't perfect athletes, but they tried hard. They responded positively to the demanding practices and the strict, disciplined conditioning. In the fifteen years of my coaching, I was blessed enough to have only one losing season and one season where we finished with the same number of wins and losses. Our teams were in championship games twelve of the fifteen years. Once my program had a forty-five game-winning streak, which is two and a half years without a loss.

My basketball team had built a tradition that wanted nothing less than a winning record, a regular-season championship, and/or tournament championships. We didn't win every championship, but we were consistently in the top two teams every year for thirteen of the fifteen years. I could not have asked the girls to commit to this program anymore than what they did. I was blessed to have other coaches who helped with practices, conditioning, and games. These coaches and players accepted me as a human being and didn't view my wheelchair as a weakness. They accepted me as a hard-nosed coach. Thus, I believe, through my physical weakness, God used me to make us all stronger, more convicted, and daily champions!

> *So keep up your courage, men, for I have faith*
> *in God that it will happen just as he told me.*
> *Acts 27:25*

Chapter Eight
The Price of Glory is High

"It's not the "will to win" that matters. Everyone has that. It's the will to prepare to win that matters."

Coach "Bear" Bryant

OVER THE YEARS of coaching, I gained the reputation of being strict – a seemingly heartless coach. Expected the girls to give their best and work the hardest they had ever worked before. Even though understanding there would be bad days and days when the girls didn't feel good, but wouldn't take any excuses for less than their best effort. If I could get up in the morning, get dressed, and go to school to teach while being in a wheelchair, then they could get their able-bodied selves up, get ready for school and prepare for practice. If one excuse was accepted, then they might push the envelope and see what other excuses I would take that would let them out of practice, working hard, or not giving their best effort.

When we were not on the court, whether it was a practice or game, I liked to have fun and enjoyed watching the girls be young kids. Not all the time did they have to experience stress because of my strict demands, but it was fun watching them before practice sing, dance, help each other with homework, play jokes among themselves, and just relax before their dedicated selves hit the floor. The girls were taught that there was a time for fun and a time to get down to business.

Even though people perceived me as being hard-nosed and strict, I did have a kind and caring heart. Making sure the girls' lives were on the right track and there were as few negatives as possible in their lives. Not only as their basketball coach, but also felt like a basketball father to them. Making sure their behavior in school was correct, keeping their grades up, and insisting they be respectful to their parents as well. By making this team, they were representing our school not only on the court but also off the court, which included the classroom, their home, the mall, or the movies. On this team, they represented the school, the coaches and their families, but most of all, themselves. We expected respectful and considerate young ladies.

In the middle school years, sometimes teenagers get that "know-it-all" attitude. They think they don't have to listen to their parents and other adults. Several times I had parents come to me and talk about their daughter's behavior and attitude at home. The girl would be disrespectful or apathetic at home, but the parents would recognize a difference when their girl was on the team and around the coaches. The parents would ask me to talk to their child about showing some respect to them and to talk to them about improving their attitude and behavior. It's amazing to me that sometimes these girls would listen to their coach before their parents. I would have a talk with the girl and explain that her parents were just that – her parents and that she needed to love them, show them respect, and have a better attitude toward her family. Her parents would always be her parents, no matter what the circumstances were during her life. After about a fifteen minute talk, the girl would look at me and promise to do better at home. Then I would say to the girl that she needed to go home, give her mother a big kiss and a hug, telling her she loved her. The girl agreed she would. Then tell her, "I will ask your mother if you did this." The next day after asking the parents; they would confirm that their daughter did. These connections and reminders proved to be very important in molding these young ladies.

In 2006, we were playing in a summer league. One night only six girls out of twelve showed up to play two games because the other team members were on vacation. Fortunately, it was our more competitive six players, and with about three minutes left before the first half of the first game, I called a timeout and told the girls to look at the scoreboard. We were winning by about thirty points because we could outrun the other team up and down the court since we were in such good condition. So during the timeout, the girls were to slow the game down so both teams could work on some offense and defense. These summer games were for instructional and fundamental improvements. If they continued running and gunning, I would take three of them out of the game and play with only two players if we needed to. We were not here to embarrass or disrespect the other team. Just because we were a better team didn't mean we had to rub it in their faces. We were going to respect the other team and the game of basketball.

The first minute or so the girls did well slowing the ball down and working on offensive plays, but all of a sudden they got a rebound, and the gates were open and the horses were all off at top speed. As they were going past me, I yelled out three of the girls' names and told them to sit on the bench. We would finish this first half with two players.

Now we had two girls on the court and four girls sitting on the bench. As the game was going on, one of the referees went past me telling me to put the girls back in the game. I said, "No."

At the next dead ball, the referee came to the girls and told them to get back in the game. Three of them stood up, and then I asked, "Girls, who coaches this team?" So they sat down. The referee didn't like my applying this discipline to my team, or I should say he didn't understand the circumstances of not following directions, so he gave me a technical foul. While the other team was shooting their free throws, the referee came to me and said those players better be on the court by the time they finished shooting free throws or he would give me a second technical foul, which meant I would be kicked out of the game. Being ejected from the building would not be a good example for the girls, so I told those three girls that they could go onto the court, stand in the corner, and not chase any basketballs around. By now, the referee was yelling in the gym that I was making fun of the game. Yelling back at the referee to look at the scoreboard, and my team was to slow down so we could work on plays and improve.

At halftime, I went to the referee to explain what was happening, and he finally understood what was going on. He thought that I was allowing my players to rest because we had only six players. Assuring him that wasn't my intention, if he still felt that way, I would have my team run during halftime so we could build our conditioning stamina. He said, no, he believed I would do that. We both apologized for the misunderstanding. At that time, those girls were mad at me, but they respected me for my discipline and teaching. Years later, that night was one of the most talked about games and one of the most laughed about situations. The girls would refer to it as one of their most memorable basketball experiences.

When our season started that fall, we were undefeated. Our next game was against the second-place team in our county. Two days before the game, I felt as if practice was as bad as a practice could be. It seemed to me that the girls were going through the motions and not taking this important game seriously enough. Leaving practice early, after getting mad, being afraid I might say something to hurt the girls' feelings, so my assistant coach finished the practice.

The first time we had played this team we were down by eleven points starting the fourth quarter. We came back to win the game by three points. Sometimes going undefeated can be a curse because the team thinks they are invincible. They think the other team will just lie down and let them run over them.

The next day practice was different from any other practice in a long time. I decided later they could enjoy some of their practice time working on what they wanted to so they could release some stress and pressure. After about half the practice, we worked on a trapping half-court defense so the girls would be more active and in motion, causing them to be more aggressive, defensively going after the ball. After that game, we beat the second-place team by thirty points. There was nothing the girls could do wrong that night. I was proud of the way the team responded to the earlier game situation and played the lights out. This team was carrying a forty-five game-winning streak. There was so much pressure on them. A lot of athletes don't get this kind of pressure in their entire career. Respect and hard work paid off.

All hard work brings a profit, but
mere talk leads only to poverty.
Proverbs 15:23

Chapter Nine
Happy Birthday to Me

*Your life is a gift from the Creator. Your gift back
to the Creator is what you do with your life.*

Billy Mills

In 1999, a teacher's assistant, Jena, came into my room before the school day started. She asked, "James, are you a Christian?"

I replied, "No. I believe people go to heaven as long as they are good. As long as they don't kill, rape, and abuse each other. I believe as long as we are good more than bad we will go to heaven."

Jena said, "I have this book for you to read. I think you will like it."

I agreed to read her book.

A few days later, Jena brought me the book in a brown paper bag. I asked, "What kind of book is this that you have to hide it in a brown bag?"

We laughed a little bit, and then she responded with, "You'll like it. I have had it in my family for years. You will see notes that I have written. Let me know when you finish. I can pass it on to other people"

I took the book and said, "Okay."

The book, brown bag and all, was placed on my bookshelf and I did not think anymore about it. Several times I would see the bag when getting a notebook off the shelf, but I did not read it.

Jena approached me to see if I had read the book about a year later. She said, "James, have you read the book I loaned you? I have someone else that could be helped by reading it."

I explained, "No, not yet. Since having it for nearly a year, I probably won't read it. I'll get it and you can let your other friend read it."

She answered, "Oh James, you go ahead and read it, and I will pass it on later."

Even though I had not really thought about the book in nearly a year, spring break was starting the following week, so I decided it was time to sit down and read.

The book was called *He Still Moves Stones* by Max Lucado. In a nutshell, it was about Jesus' life. Jesus was dead, placed in a tomb and sealed by a boulder. He came back to life and moved the stone, and the tomb was empty. Jesus wanted the world to know He was and is still alive.

While reading the book, I would cry and wonder why my accident happened the way it did. My life felt empty, and not know why. I kept looking at my past and all that I had lost. I would think about things I would never accomplish in life such as throwing a baseball again, building and climbing a tree house, or teaching my children to drive, if ever having any children.

After reading the book, I looked at the back of it and saw other books written by Max Lucado. I noticed one book, *The Applause of Heaven*, which looked familiar. After going into my sports room, there on my shelf was the book *The Applause of Heaven*. It was given to me by a student three years earlier. I read it during spring break, and now possess seventeen of Max Lucado's books. Looking back, Jena and her book was the kick start of my becoming a Christian.

In the spring of 2000, while teaching class one day, one of my students said that her church youth group was talking about why bad things happen to good people. I wished I knew; they were talking about something that I would like to hear. She informed me that they just introduced the topic that week, and next week they would be discussing it. So she invited me to her church youth group.

The following week I went to First Baptist Church of Hendersonville. When first entering, embarrassed, wondering if I would be the only adult in the youth class, listening to Paul, the Youth Minister. My student introduced me to Paul before getting started. He was excited about me being there; it was obvious Paul was told, or we could say "warned," I was going to be there that night.

It was an uplifting night. The praise and worship was awesome. Watching the youth getting involved, fired-up, and preparing for the coming of the Lord was moving. As Paul was speaking, all eyes, ears, and hearts were on him.

Paul said, "We don't live in a perfect world – it's full of sins."

Talking to myself, "That's what I believe."

Then Paul said, "God gives us free will or free choices in our lives."

Again I said, "That's what I believe."

Paul continued, "Sometimes things happen in our lives that we might not have an explanation for right now, but God knows the reason why. He will tell us or let us know when it's time."

Thinking, never thought of it that way before, but it sounded good. My heart was opening up; I started crying, but making sure no one could see me, especially the student who invited me here. Paul was talking to the whole youth group, but it seemed as if he were talking solely to me. After Paul was finished, he said if anyone wanted to talk, he would be around for awhile.

Wanting to talk with Paul, I would be nice and let all the youth get in front of me. Was I being that nice? Of course not, I didn't want people to see me if I started crying. Finally, I got to Paul. I asked him, "Why did this happen to me?"

Years earlier, I was told that God wanted to show he had control over me and that my injury happened because of my sins. Paul's answer was the best. He told me, "I don't know."

"I don't know." What kind of an answer is that? "I don't know." Then it hit me. It was the truth. Paul doesn't know why, I don't know why, but God knows exactly why. I may never know why until God wants me to know.

Crying to Paul like a man should never cry to a stranger, I was crying like a baby or a man missing his Father. That night Paul asked me if I wanted to be saved.

I told Paul, "I'm not worthy of being saved."

Paul said, "None of us are worthy of saving."

I said, "I'm too bad of a person."

Paul said, "None of us are good enough to be saved. We deserve hell, but because of the grace of God, we can be saved."

Jesus was working to get me saved; satan was working equally hard on me. That night I didn't get saved. Paul prayed and called it a night.

For the next two months, I was going to school putting on a face – a front. But on the way home, I would cry while driving. On Sundays, *Touched By An Angel* would come on. While watching, I would cry. Attending church during this time, but not a member, one Sunday, the preacher said that the church was taking a few buses downtown Nashville to Adelphia Coliseum, the home of the Tennessee Titans. Billy Graham was preaching there.

I asked the minister, "Is the bus handicapped accessible?"

He said, "No." But he would find another way for me to go. He never contacted me to tell me the plan on how to get there. One crusade night, I listened to Billy Graham on the internet by streaming. Technology is great, but it didn't seem the same. On the last night of the crusade, I drove myself, and my fellow coach, Rick, met me there to make sure I got in safely.

When arriving at the coliseum, I was sitting beside a man in a wheelchair. We were talking, and he told me he was from Germany. He was here visiting from a rehabilitation center in Atlanta. He told me that he was in Atlanta and heard on the radio about Billy Graham being in Nashville. He rode a bus and taxi to get to Nashville. Then he told me that people won't believe it. I asked, "Believe what?" He said people in Germany won't believe that he was in a stadium where there were 70,000 people in one building who came to listen to one person talk about religion. That statement just amazed me.

Billy Graham's message was about the fall of man, how God gave humans free choice, how we as humans deserve hell, but God gave us a way out because of God's son, Jesus. I started thinking that, this was the same message that Paul gave. As Billy Graham was talking, my heart was having a strange feeling. The love of God, strength and courage never felt before. Hope was given to me that, when I get to heaven, there would be no more pain, no more feelings of rejection, no more depression, and no more wheelchairs. Where we are now, here on earth, is a temporary place. The everlasting eternity that we will spend in heaven with our Heavenly Father is what we should be waiting for. Billy Graham went on saying there was no way we can earn our way to heaven. We can never be good enough; we can never buy or earn our way to heaven. The only way we can get to heaven is to be saved by receiving and believing Jesus is our Lord and Savior, confessing our sins, and repenting from our sins. As Billy Graham was speaking, I was praying to receive Jesus in my heart. I was feeling the Holy Ghost in my heart and soul.

There was an invitation to the public to come forward to receive Jesus. As going forward, Coach Rick saw me from a distance. He made his way from the seats and worked through the crowd to be with me. Later, I found out some of my students and players were there and witnessed my profession.

My students usually asked me, "Coach, when is your birthday?"

I like celebrating birthdays as much as anyone else. I respond to my students that my birthday is June 4; June 12; July 9; and September 11. By this time, my students are laughing and wondering what am I talking about, and again they ask me, "Coach, when is your birthday?"

This time I go, "Oh, you mean my birthday."

They're still laughing and respond, "Yes, your birthday."

I respond with, "June 4; June 12; July 9; and September 11." Now that I have my students' attention, they're no longer laughing but are waiting eagerly to understand how I have so many birthdays.

June 4, Billy Graham came to the Titans Coliseum, and that night I received Jesus as my Lord and Savior and became a new person because the Bible tells us that when we receive Christ that we are new and our old self is no longer. Even though we are saved, that doesn't mean we're perfect people. We still have bad days as well as good days. To discourage us, satan will do whatever he can. God will never put a bad or negative thought in our heads, but satan will, and he will have us believe the thought came from God.

June 12, my mother physically gave birth to me. It was time for me to make an entrance into the world. When I was born, I was as bald as a baby could be. My mother told me that I was a beautiful, bald baby boy.

July 9, is my baptism day. We went to the swimming pool and my friends and family witnessed my outward expression of receiving Jesus as my Lord and Savior. The old me was gone while the new me was beginning a new journey in life.

September 11, was the day that my life in a wheelchair began. The old life of being athlete, supporter, provider, and even walker came to a stop. That was the day I sustained a spinal cord injury playing football. Another person hit me high and unexpectedly; the tackle came after scoring a touchdown. The hit severed three vertebrae in my neck.

My students at the beginning of the school year ask about my injury. Not wanting them to be afraid of me and my wheelchair. This statement might be hard to believe, but my injury was one of the best things that could have happened to me. Yes, of course, I wanted to be in the pros, but in reality less than one percent of athletes make it to the pros. So who knows? If it wasn't for my injury, I might be homeless, living under a river bridge and wondering where my next meal would be coming from.

Today, after completing my master's degree, teach and coach our girls' basketball team, but, most importantly, I have a relationship with Jesus. When this old body dies, I'll be with Jesus.

If it were not for my injury, having a relationship with Jesus might not have been possible, because of believing I was invincible. Believing my success came from my hard work, my desire, my determination, not from God who gave me the talent to play baseball.

There is only one thing that I regret about that day. My family had to suffer with me. They have gone through every experience with me including my pain and sorrow.

There are four reasons that contribute to my success in life:

1. God in my life.
2. My family – God knew I needed this family years before I was even thought of here on earth.
3. Friends – Whom God placed in my life to encourage, push, and never give up on me.
4. Attitude – The hard work, desire, and determination that God gave me before I was born.

In life we have choices to make. There are going to be crossroads in our lives. God knows the roads we will travel, but gives us the free will to decide what we want to do with our lives. Most of the time, we choose the right road to travel, but sometimes we choose the wrong road. Something bad might happen. Then we feel that we were dealt a bad hand, we were given lemons to eat, or were just downright double-crossed.

There are times that we take the correct road in life, but then we have to live because of someone else's poor decision. I was playing an innocent game of football, and someone else decided to play carelessly. Now, living my life in a wheelchair because of the choice he made. Maybe you're going to church one day, the correct road to take, but a drunk driver hits your family's car and changes your life forever. We have a choice in how we will react to the situations in our lives.

Sometimes we make choices in life that are good ones, sometimes bad ones, and sometimes others make wrong choices that affect us. Anyway, we must go forward from those choices. We can feel angry and bitter about life, or we can play out our hands, make lemonade or pray for our attitude to be positive. Then we can make the best out of any situation.

My students sometimes look at me and ask if that was a good day, the day of the injury, then what was my worst day? I look at them and say, "The same day."

Therefore, if anyone is in Christ, the new creation has come: The old has gone, the new is here!
2 Corinthians 5:17

Chapter Ten
I'm Going Where?

*Take the first step in faith. You don't have to
see the whole staircase, just take the first step.*
Martin Luther King, Jr.

IN THE FALL of 2000, I made a decision to travel to Africa the following summer. Actually, going to the Comoro Islands, four islands located between the east coast of Africa and Madagascar. The group was going to teach some sports – baseball, basketball, and soccer. While we were there, I would be showing, demonstrating and educating the people that individuals with disabilities should be out of their houses and in the public. In that part of the world, people who were disabled weren't allowed in public if they couldn't do anything to provide for or help support their community. They stayed in their houses – out of sight, out of mind. Feeling this was an opportunity to help other people get out of their homes and show they can be productive in society. I needed this challenge in my life, so I signed up.

Not having the funds to travel, I began writing letters to my former basketball players' families and friends asking for their assistance. I asked people to pray about the trip and if they could, to provide donations to help me raise funds for the trip. People were very generous and helpful in many ways, encouraging me to go.

On Thursday, April 5, 2001, approximately one hundred letters were sent to people asking for their prayers and financial assistance. God was at work. People were responding generously. I received nothing but encouragement and praise for my destination, even though some people voiced concern for my travel considerations, and also security concerns about that part of the world. The main reason for their concern was my health overseas. Due to being a quadriplegic, one major problem anticipated was urinary tract infections. The nerve signals that cause my bladder to release urine don't function properly. Therefore, bacteria build up in the unreleased urine can cause an infection that requires antibiotics.

Another concern was hyperreflexia, common among individuals with spinal cord injuries. The body shakes uncontrollably as if freezing. It is accompanied by headaches because the blood pressure is rising. To resolve this issue, I lie in bed with multiple blankets and cover myself from head to toe. This process takes about four hours. Afterwards, I slowly remove covers because I'm too hot. If the blankets are removed too fast, I cool off too fast and have to start the procedure over. Usually this happens when I go three or four nights without good sleep. It's the body's way of telling me that I need to slow down to recover from exertion. When it was closer to departure time, I met with my doctor who prescribed a daily antibiotic that would help prevent urine infections. I had to stay aware of the signals my body gave so I would know when I needed sleep. I couldn't wait to see God in action.

In the middle of April, money was coming in, and people were excited about my going to Africa. People would reinforce that funding for my trip was on the way. I needed $1,500 by May 13 and close to $2,600 by the end of May. As more checks were coming, I was prepared for my traveling adventure. A few places donated school supplies to be given to the children there.

In May, there was $1,475 in my account and I needed a total of $1,500 by the middle of the month to secure my deposit. This was about half of what was needed to make the trip. Marty, a spiritual friend of mine, meets once a month with members of his church for a men's breakfast. I was asked earlier in April to talk with the men's group about my voyage. While speaking with Marty's group, I told them about the $1,475 already received and that I needed $25 to meet my first goal by May 13, the next day.

They didn't know about my funds, but they had met an hour before I got there and collected $25 for my trip. This was more confirmation: God is always at work! They collected the exact amount of money I needed, and they were not aware that I would mention funds at all. God laid it on their hearts to contribute and look what happened – I met my first goal. Thank you, Lord.

Three checks came in to put me over my $2,600 that was needed by the end of May – Praise God. Any money received over the necessary amount was added to other people's funds to help them achieve their goal. Not only did people help me achieve my target, but they also helped others as well.

In the middle of June, I called a few medical supply stores asking for donations of wheelchairs, walkers, or cushions so that the people with disabilities in Africa could get around easier in their community.

Ed Medical Supplies called and said they were doing their end of the year inventory and that they had a thirty yard long dumpster with wheelchairs, parts, walkers, and even a bed in it. I could have all I wanted. I just needed to dumpster dive and retrieve any items I desired.

A friend of mine, Bruce, went with me to Ed Medical. Bruce climbed up in the dumpster and brought out twelve wheelchairs. Two or three were brand new while others were used. There were plenty of parts to help rebuild some wheelchairs. Thank God for Bruce. I told him I would pay for his gas, but he said no, this was his way of contributing to God's work.

The third week of June, Rick and I had our summer basketball camp. After camp one afternoon, Rick drove me and we picked up two more wheelchairs and more parts to take on the trip. Rick dove in the dumpster as if he had done this before. Thank you God for Rick being my friend. I'm so blessed to have him as a friend and brother in Christ.

The day before leaving for Africa, Bear was helping me pack my bags. My family and friends had been giving helpful advice and support. They were proud of me that I was going to help others with disabilities and prove that a person with a disability can be functional in society. They advised me to demonstrate to the people around the world that even though some people have disabilities, they can be successful, productive, and provide a positive atmosphere for the community. Thank you God for my family and friends.

Thursday, June 21, was travel day. I slept well that night even though being excited. I met with my family to eat breakfast, kissed my mother good-bye, told Bear and Andy bye, and assured them of my love. Bear drove me to the airport. I was nervous, but it was a good feeling because I had confidence that God had taken control and all would be prepared for us. I told Bear bye and I loved him.

Since being in a wheelchair, I boarded the plane first. I had to get out of my wheelchair because the aisles on the plane were too narrow, and was placed on a cart. When my seat was located I was helped over to it and seat belted in. It was fun watching people maneuver around the plane and watching members of the group taking their seats with excitement.

Our first stop was only a forty-five minute flight to Atlanta. The flight was good. While getting on the plane first, I was the last to get off. After we got there, we exited the plane and went to the next plane that was bound for Paris. Atlanta airport was huge. We had only about thirty minutes to get to the next plane. Different people from the group helped push me so we could get to the plane in time. It was the same procedure getting on the plane as earlier.

Flying to Paris took eight hours. Looking out the window and seeing the ocean was remarkable. I could not sleep sitting up, so I watched *Miss Congeniality*, not once, but twice and praying about the flight.

We spent the next ten hours in Paris. When we got off the plane, a person at the airport was checking passports. He looked at me but asked someone else about my credentials. I told him I could answer his questions. He looked at me, then turned to the other person, and proceeded questioning my passport with him.

I wondered if this trip was going to be a mistake. Knowing people would help me, but I didn't think it would be so much help – work. I figured on needing help up one, two, or even three steps, but not carrying me up thirty or even fifty steps at a time, not once, twice, but at least ten times up or down stairs or escalators. Being a big and heavy person, I was worried about hurting someone from all the lifting. No one in our group ever complained about helping me. I did a lot of praying to God for relief and assurance.

Seeing the Eiffel Tower was huge and amazing. Since the tower was not handicap accessible, different people from the group took my cameras with them and took pictures. They did not want me to miss out on what they were experiencing.

There were no ramps to get inside Notre Dame so I got to view it from the outside. This was a good thing at the time because one of my wheels went flat. It was hard for me to push around so I sat back and enjoyed the ride provided by different members of the group. Before leaving the states, a friend of mine, Donnie, advised me to take extra tubes and tires in case of an emergency. We found someone who could fix my wheel when we got to the hotel. Despite the small setback, the buildings and other structures were amazing to view. It's hard to believe that these buildings were constructed as beautifully as they were due to the technology back then. We ended up taking a boat ride to see the rest of Paris because of the lack of time we had. It is a special place to visit.

The men gathered around me every opportunity to make sure I could see and experience all of what they experienced. Their love for me by helping was an answered prayer. So satan had to take a back seat to my emotions toward others helping me. God is in control. I decided I would not feel guilty about the trip again. This was not a mistake.

When we were riding the train, we didn't get off at the right place for the airport. So we had to travel the distance to the end and double back, almost missing our plane. I had been up for about thirty-six hours. Power naps were impossible; all I could get was three or four minutes of shuteye at a time.

We got to the airport just in time to get on the plane. I was the last person on and was taken behind a partition to be searched. After watching movies, I thought they were going to strip-search me. Two airport guards came in to search me so I started taking off my shirt. They started saying "no" real fast. They checked me and my wheelchair, finding nothing suspicious, on my way to the plane.

Because of being late and the rush of getting the flight started, I was seated in first class – yes – first class. Everyone should try it just once. Recliners were passenger seats, food was better, and the pilot interacted with the people. Before the meals, the stewardess handed a hot washcloth to clean my face and hands. I could now lean back and get some sleep.

There was a man who was assigned to take special care of me. I asked if he could be with me so he could help. No problem, he was placed in first class. This person seemed to make me his own special assignment. He was making sure I was as comfortable as possible. God surely knew how to prepare this situation. Not only catching up on some needed sleep, but also have my helper in place to better prepare the future of the trip. I said, "Thank you, God," as I was nodding off.

Before we knew it, it was Saturday. After about six hours of flight, we had another layover, this time in Yemen. When I was getting on and off the planes in America and at Paris, the tunnels were level with the plane and airport, but not at Yemen. There were steps that went down from the plane to the ground. I was carried in my wheelchair down the steps. It took four or five men to carry me. The steps were steep, and the event was long. Knowing I was in good hands, but satan started in my mind about the possibility of someone getting hurt carrying me down these steps. But God gave me peace of mind and confidence in

One More Play

knowing the team of men was working to help me. They were praising each other and asking God for safety.

The Yemen airport looked like a battle zone. All the airport guards wore military attire and had weapons – guns. The airport was small, hot, crowded, and it didn't feel or seem friendly. Fortunately, our layover was only about three hours (on the way back we were going to have seventeen hours layover in Yemen – this was not going to be easy or fun.)

Leaving Yemen was an adventure, mainly due in part by getting me back on the plane. The same group of men lifted me and my wheelchair and worked as a team to get me up the stairs. This procedure would take longer going up than down where gravity surely took its toll. Again, the men made me feel blessed that I was with them. No one complained about helping but made themselves available to make sure I was on board. This way of getting on and off the plane would be repeated the rest of the trip. We were about four hours from our destination, the Comoro Islands.

We arrived at the Comoro Islands, a total of four islands, and had the privilege of staying on two of the islands. The first one was the Grande Comore, and the second island was Anjouan. It was winter time there, and thankfully, it was easily over ninety degrees.

The people of the Grande Comore were excited to see us. As we got off the plane, we were greeted with smiles, hugs, and enthusiasm by people because of all the Americans on their island. It was late in the day and getting dark. We had just enough time for dinner and a brief meeting with the coordinator of the trip. Then it was off to our rooms and much needed sleep.

I had gotten four hours of sleep in forty hours, so I made the best of the next ten hours of sleep. Thank you God, for getting us here safely and your guidance for preparing the way even before we embarked on our journey.

The sleep was great, refreshing, and just what the doctor ordered on a beautiful Sunday. I got up about ten o'clock in the morning and had a late breakfast. I wanted to take a shower but the tub was not accessible. I needed a bench to sit on because sitting on the bottom of the tub would take too much work to get out.

I met Scott. His African name was not easily remembered or pronounced. So Scott it was. Scott was from Zimbabwe, located in South Africa. He was the one that fixed my flat on my wheelchair and he cut a three-quarter inch thick plywood to construct a bench for showering purposes.

Scott used forearm crutches known as Canada crutches. I inquired about his disability. He contracted polio at the age of seven. He used a wheelchair when possible but mostly when he played wheelchair basketball. I felt blessed to have met Scott and to have seen that he could get out in public. I later found out that Scott was a vibrant Christian.

I noticed that there were no other people with disabilities out in public. I was educated about this problem earlier. Scott told me about another man in his village who was questioning him about his disability. This man believed Scott made the gods – yes, plural – "the gods" mad for some reason, and they

One More Play

made this disease infect his body. Scott believed a disability was a random act, not punishment. About seven years later, this same man was working on a roof and fell off and broke his neck. Scott visited him and reminded him of their conversation about angering the gods and asked if he believed that he got the gods mad and caused his disability. No, it was a freak accident that happened with no reasoning, the man now believed.

Later that day, the task was to put together two basketball goals; since my hands and arms don't work that well, I got to supervise. I used to work on cars with my father when I was younger. Even though I could not actually physically build these portable goals, I was mechanically minded enough to help problem solve and make suggestions. I have to admit though, putting these goals together, was a little like putting jigsaw puzzles together. Since we were to teach them how to play basketball, we had to assemble portable goals at each location. When we left the island, we left the goals behind and some new basketballs as well.

The following day, we started the day with practice. I was coaching the women's team. We had only seven women on our team with three of them former players from my middle school team. Two other women made it clear to me that they would play only if I needed them to get in the game. Since I was there to help promote people with disabilities, I had Scott join our team, and he played in his wheelchair. Scott only got in the game in the last three minutes because this was the women's game.

We practiced outdoors on asphalt with two goals at each end, much like basketball goals one could find at any park and recreation area back home. While we were practicing, we were giving basketball mini camps as well. We practiced for about an hour. People were standing in line to start the clinic. There were about seventy-five people participating, some for the first time and some who had played before. Both ends of the asphalt court were busy with people learning and having fun. Other members on the trip were giving camps on baseball and soccer at different locations.

The schedule for the games allowed us to play every third night. The first night we played against one of the Grande Comore ladies team. We didn't start playing until almost 8 P.M. We got to the arena about 6:30 in the evening to warm up and get used to the court.

The arena was something in itself. It was outdoors with twenty foot high walls surrounding it. We had to go through two doorways, similar to those on a submarine. We had to step over the doorway, or I had to be picked up, wheelchair and all, over the extended door jam. One door allowed us to come in from the outside area. The other doorway let us onto the court.

The court was open under the stars. The floor of the court was concrete with paint to provide the basketball court perimeters. Even though they used a dust mop, it was still slippery, like playing on glass. People were slip sliding away. I was worried about somebody getting hurt. Before the game started, I was taking in the enthusiasm of the people that came to watch the game. There must have been 600 people in the stands with another seventy-five people sitting or standing on the twenty foot high wall. I don't know if people paid to watch us play but some would say it was a "sold out" crowd.

We played the Comoro Ladies. They were older than we were and seemed to have been playing as a team for a long time. We had three girls who were still in high school, one who had just graduated high school, one who played college basketball, and the other two – were fine with just sitting, and playing only if needed. We had only been a team for less than a week and seemed to be out-matched. Before the game started, I was advised not only to win the game but also to win as big as possible. It was a tough game, and we prevailed by winning forty-three to thirty-nine. My first international victory as a coach came that night.

When all games were finished, it was about 1 o'clock in the morning. Everybody in the stands and the ones sitting on top of the wall flooded the court to shake hands with the Americans and get a chance to talk with us. It was exciting and chaotic at the same time. The Comoro people were rushing to every one of us to get information about our lives, but I noticed not everyone was being overwhelmed. That one person was me. I then got to experience what Scott was telling me about individuals with disabilities in this country. If you can't contribute by being productive in society, then you're not expected to be in the public eye. Even though I coached the women's team to victory, it wasn't possible to get the same respect as an able-bodied person. Don't get me wrong. I was glad for the others, especially the younger group of people, but it was discouraging for me. People here were viewing my disability rather than making an effort to know me as a person, a human being. We finally got on the bus and got back to our rooms about 2 A.M. That was a long day.

On Tuesday, June 26, we slept in and got up around 9 or 10 A.M. A special event was planned for us. We were going to the governor's house to meet him. Their term 'governor' means the president of the country of the four islands. We were told to wear our gray sport polo shirts with our long navy blue sweat pants so we would match as a group. The mansion was beautiful and on top a hill. People helped me up the stairs, into the building, to experience this once-in-a-lifetime event.

I have never met a president before and probably will never meet one again, but I was electrified by the anticipation. Scott and I had been in the front row talking about forty-five minutes when we noticed a parade of people coming down the stairs, from the floor above us. There was an entourage of people who presented the governor to us. The group was welcomed to the Grande Comore and the other islands. We were acknowledged as being the largest sporting group from America to ever visit the islands.

Scott and I were brought forward to meet the governor personally. He recognized us for having a disability, but not allowing our challenges limit us as people. We were encouraged to continue overcoming adversities and to be ambassadors for other people with disabilities. The governor wanted to break old stigmas about people with disabilities and set new standards for individuals with disabilities to follow. After last night, being ignored because of my disability, this was a positive atmosphere with the governor encouraging his people who have disabilities to actually participate in the community. It would be a long road, but Scott and I could start making a difference for the disabled by being present and active in the Comoro society.

The ladies and I had the night off, so we watched the men play two games. There were a lot of people trying to talk and get to know the women, but no one came to talk with me. After meeting the president, I was wondering what I needed to do to help the people with disabilities here. Again, I didn't see anyone else, other than Scott, with disabilities. I didn't know what to do, so I prayed. "Lord, let me know how I can encourage and be an example for all people here, not just the ones with disabilities. Amen."

Watch out what you pray for, because you might not know how or what will happen to answer that prayer. After watching the men play both games, with both American groups winning, the crowd swarmed the court in pursuit of an American conversation. Again, I watched other people getting interviewed and idolized for being American, and yet I was ignored. Finally, we made our way out to catch the bus to take us back to our motel.

As we were waiting for our ride, a man came to me who seemed to be mentally challenged or drunk, and in his broken English conveyed to me he wanted to know my religion. When the bus got there, he not only helped me on but he also jumped on with me. He apparently thought he was going to America.

He sat beside me with confidence, thinking he was leaving his situation and going to a better opportunity in life. Moments later, he was escorted off the bus and I never saw him again.

The next morning we got up and had breakfast. Later, before noon, we went to lead a few camps for the people. They could choose to participate in basketball, baseball, or soccer. From what I could see, they could teach us a thing or two about soccer. They were running bare footed and moving the ball quicker than I had ever seen. The camps went great and lasted about three hours. We got back to our rooms so we could recover for the games that night.

We got to the arena about 6:30 P.M. so we could warm up and get the feeling of the atmosphere from the Comoro crowd. It was electrifying again. It was much like the first night we played. We played the Comoro Ladies International team. They were better than the Grande Comore Ladies and seemed to be more athletic. Again, we had our five basketball players, two women who would play only if needed, and Scott in his wheelchair.

Before the game, I was informed that Scott would not be allowed to play because the other team didn't know how to defend him. They felt it would be unfair. With about six minutes left in the game, one of my starters fouled out. It was time for one of the others to get some experience on the court. This would really be hands-on training. After about four trips up and down the court, our newly reserved player was ready to pass out. I called a time out and told her to stay on the defensive side of the court and not to worry about offense. She answered to this coaching strategy with "Praise the Lord."

We played four on five offensively while allowing the sub to gain her strength and confidence on the defensive side. When the game ended, the final score was forty-nine to forty-five. We won. How about that? We won two games in international play. Coaching doesn't get better than this or any more fun than this. Thank you Lord, for allowing me to have a few more games with my former players.

After the game, I was looking around the arena and spotted two people with disabilities. One used forearm crutches, and the other was in a wheelchair. They were there to see what people with disabilities can do. I told them about my teaching and coaching career, also informed them that many individuals with disabilities in America are active in their communities. Not all people in America with disabilities are employed, but a lot of them help by volunteering. The look in these people's eyes let me know they wanted more respect, encouragement, and acceptance from their own people.

After the men's game, the same controlled chaos took place, but this time more people were talking with me. They wanted to know more about how American people treat the disabled. After we had won two games, their eyes and minds were opened. They could not believe that I was able to contribute to basketball, since I could not get up and walk or demonstrate the game. Although my legs don't work, my mind does. They seemed to accept me as the week went by, which was not a minute too late. When we returned to our rooms around two in the morning, I whispered, "Thank you Lord, for giving me the opportunity to plant seeds. I pray we have helped those with disabilities. May they be acknowledged as individuals and recognized for their involvement in this country." The next morning we got up early and packed our bags to fly to Anjouan.

> *Trust in the LORD and do good; dwell in the land and enjoy safe pasture.*
> *Psalms 37:3*

Chapter Eleven
Anjouan, Here We Come

Do not go where the path may lead, go instead where there is no path and leave a trail.

Ralph Waldo Emerson

On June 28, I was not ready to leave paradise, the Grande Comore, but it was time to travel to our next destination, Anjouan. The view outside my hotel room was heavenly, the blue ocean blanket covered the white sandy beach, and at the same time the blue water was clashing against the rough jagged edges of the cliff. There was a nice calm breeze that had the smell of the beach and ocean combined.

As I was sitting on a cliff, I saw from a distance, on the cliff across from me, the two portable basketball goals that we had brought from America, I had helped to construct, were left for the people. I couldn't help thinking; we were treated like kings and queens by the Grande Comore residents, no matter where we traveled or where we gather. I was sleepy because we had gotten up about 6 A.M. and had only four hours' sleep in order to make our way to Anjouan, the next paradise island on our journey's end.

We arrived at the airport about 7:30 in the morning with one concern – we weren't flying on a major airline, but a charter plane that held around twenty people. We had to divide into two groups. All of us had to tell our weight, which included my wheelchair, and all bags were weighed as well. The first group finally left about 9 A.M. taking roughly forty-five minutes to reach Anjouan. That meant the second group had to wait over an hour and a half for the plane to make its round trip flight, plus the unloading of the first group. I was with the second group to fly over. We waited patiently for our opportunity to board the small plane so we could be together with our other team members.

I was picked up, wheelchair and all, so I could get on this little plane. After getting me in, I stood up and sat on the plane's seat and my wheelchair was loaded with the other baggage. It seemed crowded, and I had concerns about this flight. I had never been on a plane this small. The flight was bumpy and rough. Even though I was seat-belted in, I was sliding side to side, and the turbulence caused the plane to rock, but the pilot was having a good time letting us know – no problem. He sat the plane down as smooth as glass.

It was my understanding that rarely do Americans travel to the island of Anjouan. When we were getting off the plane, we were given pretty, fragrant leis as presents. The leis were surprisingly heavier than I thought they would be. We were welcomed with tribal dancing and celebrating. Watching their ritual rejoicing with enthusiasm was entertaining, and I had a sense of peaceful relaxation and enjoyment. As soon as we left the airport, there was a parade. Basically we were the parade. We were escorted in several automobiles that drove us around town three or four times with people waving and cheering. People were standing next to the road with excitement, seeming to have a roadside party because of us.

I noticed as we were traveling to our hotel, as Dorothy would say, "We're not in Kansas anymore." Anjouan was very different than the Grande Comore. First, there wasn't the nice breeze we previously had; it was much hotter and more humid. It's a good thing that it was winter here because it was constantly 90+ degrees. I don't sweat from my neck down, due to my spinal cord injury, making it feet like 98+ degrees. It became necessary to pour bottled water over my body to cool down. I needed to get to the hotel so my body could recover with the air conditioner.

Secondly, it looked as if we were going through a war zone. There were abandoned buildings and houses, roads with huge holes and little pavement. Automobiles were on the side of the road; some of the cars were on blocks, and others were stripped so that all you could see were the frames. Overall, Anjouan seemed to be poorer and less attractive compared to the Grande Comore.

It was about one in the afternoon when I noticed the electricity went off, which meant no air conditioner at this time. I stayed underneath a shaded area waiting for the beach breeze to begin, but none came. So I kept pouring water and fanning myself. About an hour and a half went by and the electricity hadn't come on yet. Asking about the problem, I was informed the electricity would be back on around 5 P.M. and would be off again between 2 A.M. and 7 A.M. Clocks could be set by the power outage and return. My understanding was the electricity is preserved daily so power could be used to supply the people throughout the month. In households and businesses, except for the government facilities, electricity was shut down between these hours, even if the bill was paid for the month.

There were no basketball games that first night. This break allowed all the athletes, coaches, and referees to recover from night after night of play and day camps. We got to enjoy the Anjouan committee activities. We were taken to meet the mayor of Anjouan and have dinner with him. There must have been seventy-five steps to get up to the mayor's office. I was carried up the steps, along with my wheelchair, by a group of men. People were watching how I was treated, and it seemed to me that they thought I was treated like a king; heck, I was being carried like a king. When we went up to the office or back to the ground floor, a group of men made sure I was taken care of. The experience of love the men poured out on me was overwhelming. I thought about doing my Titanic expression, putting my hands up and shouting, "I'm king of the world," but I didn't.

The mayor acknowledged our presence on the island and again brought the attention to Scott and myself for not allowing our disabilities to slow us down. The mayor wanted to use Scott and me as examples for the Anjouan community, to encourage people with disabilities to take part in society.

Before we traveled to the Comoro Islands, we were required to take medication to help prevent getting malaria. I had to take it a week before we left for the islands, while I was there, and then a week after returning to the states. It was recommended that we also apply mosquito spray with DEET thirty. On the Grande Comore, we didn't think of malaria because we slept with our windows and doors closed while the air conditioning was pouring out the cold air. But on Anjouan, malaria was a common concern. With the electricity outage at two in the morning every night, we had to sleep under a net with the windows open while saturated in DEET to discourage infected mosquitoes. As I was lying in bed that first night, I recalled the prior paradise and now God was telling me to trust in Him in hard times, saying, "I'll be there watching over you, when you think you're alone, I'll open your eyes to all." I believed I would learn more from this island than the first one, and the final experience would be more rewarding as well.

The next day, Friday, I got hot when the electricity was turned off at night. It was uncomfortable without the air conditioner, but I was able to sleep because of exhaustion. I got up when the power was restored, in time to get a shower and get ready for breakfast. We kept the same routine, providing sports camps during the morning until lunch, then going back to the hotel to relax, and playing basketball games throughout the evening.

The ladies had their first game around 8 P.M. Earlier in the afternoon, I prayed for rain because it was so hot, the power was off, and I needed a breeze to stay cooled. God provided heavy rainfall and strong winds to deliver His natural air conditioner. "Thank you, God. The timing was just right, just like all of your answered prayers."

While I had this nice break, I started thinking about Scott and how to use him in our games. Scott wouldn't be allowed to play, so what could he do to show off his disability as a real ability? Then it came to me – "Thank you, God," that Scott could demonstrate his basketball skills during half time of our game. Scott agreed with the suggestion to perform his talents on the court.

The arena was a little different from where we played the first two games; we played on asphalt that was open to the world. There were no high walls or fences to keep us in or other people out. The seating arrangement had bleachers, and it was standing room only. The scoreboard was kept by hand. When a team scored, someone would remove the score and put up the new score (people at Wrigley Field would have been proud.) The clock had hands on it to count down both halves of the game. The perimeter of the basketball court had just been painted. I rolled over the court and wet paint was on my tires and hands. The simplicity of where we were to play brought back my childhood days of recreation, and the innocence of playing in the neighborhood.

At half time, we were struggling against a good team, but it was time for Scott to demonstrate his gift. He had several basketballs strategically placed on the court so he could perform his ball handling skills. Scott pushed up to a basketball and without stopping, he leaned to his right and pushed a ball against his right wheel. The ball rode up the rotation of his wheel until he could grab the ball and take it for a layup. Scott took some shots and knocked down a few three pointers making the crowd go ballistic. Scott represented people with disabilities heroically, gaining respect from his country.

The game was thrilling but too close, because we were losing for the first time by one point, with fewer than three minutes left in the game. I witnessed my former middle school girls grow up that night, to be competitive strong women basketball players. My point guard became the leader; I always knew she could be. She thumped a few threes to keep us in the game. My wing player moved to a post-position to cover for the player that fouled out. She played like she was meant to be there. She put herself into position to get key rebounds that limited the other team on second chances. The other post player stepped up her game with key rebounds and assists. She made a few free throws to ice the game with forty seconds left in the game. When the game ended, the final score was forty to thirty-nine. We won. How about that? We remained undefeated with a record of three wins and no losses. "Thank you God." (again, for the privilege of being with these ladies as basketball players and observing their strength as witnesses for your kingdom.)

While heading to the basketball court for camps on that Saturday, we went to another part of the island, where we would finish our tour playing the other Comoro teams. The court was like the court from the Grande Comore. The outdoor court was slippery as glass, and it seemed even harder to maintain control on this court. Worry again consumed me that someone might get hurt. To top it all off, my body was once again overheated. Pouring water over my body to stay cool was a temporary solution, but I was warming up too fast. People noticed how hot I was and brought me an umbrella to keep me from being in direct sunlight. The humidity was high and the water I applied evaporated quickly. I finally got back to the room and rested in order to cool down. After about two hours, I felt better and got ready for the men's game.

Since it was hot the next day, I decided to stay at the hotel instead of helping with the camps. I had to take care of my health, so I would not get sick from the heat, and besides, we would be going to America the next day. The experience had been awe-inspiring, but it was time to go home. The ladies played that night and I needed to be as healthy as possible so I could finish the tour with the team.

We got to the playing area, and I noticed about forty children waiting for us. As I was getting out of the vehicle, one of the children asked me my name and what I did in America.

I replied, "My name is James. I teach science and coach basketball back home."

The interpreter relayed my answer to the crowd in their language, and there was a surprising "Awe." They couldn't believe I was really a teacher and a coach. Not only were they watching me coach, but they were also cheering for the team.

The game started on time, as more people came to watch. We had a comfortable half time lead, and Scott performed his ball skills to perfection. Also, during half time, there was a ceremony that recognized a few folks with disabilities. They were presented with wheelchairs, brought from America. It was humbling watching the gratitude of the much-deserving individuals. These gifts would help them gain independence and self-worth. I thanked God for allowing me to be a small part of their transformation. And also silently thanked God for my friend, Bruce and Rick who gave of their time to "dumpster dive" for souls in Africa.

During the second half, my concern for someone getting hurt was fulfilled. My point guard went down on the slippery court trying for a steal and hurt her left arm. I was encouraging her to keep playing, trying to convince her she was not hurt that bad. I didn't call a timeout. After the third trip back down to play defense, she looked at me trying not to cry, but I could tell her arm was hurting. Her left arm hung there lifeless. I called the necessary timeout. As she was coming off the court, she looked worried. She was taken to get an x-ray, which we found out later wasn't working. Someone made a duct tape sling to help keep her arm up right and make it as comfortable as possible.

With her out of the game, I prayed with the team asking God for His protection over her injury. If there was a break, that it would be a clean break, so it would heal correctly. We went to our game plan playing with four people on offense and five on defense. My mighty sub was to play defense and no offense. This would relieve her from running up and down the court saving her full strength for defense. Like before, her response was, "Amen." We won by fifteen points and finished undefeated, four wins with zero losses, respectfully representing ourselves, and the Lord. After the game, we focused our attention on the injured player.

She didn't get much sleep due to the pain. The other girls took care of her like a mother would care for her daughter. They helped her prepare for our trip home, while making her as comfortable as possible. They helped dress her, carried her plate of food to the table, and stayed by her side to protect her from any accidental bumping of her arm. She had her own personal entourage.

About 10 A.M. on July 2nd, we boarded a charter plane to make our way back to U.S.A. Our first stop was a layover on the Grande Comore. We had an eight-hour stop to relax, clean up, finish packing, and say good-bye to our friends. When we got to the Grande Comore, we were taken to a different hotel. I was disappointed, because I wanted to sit on that cliff again and take in the ultimate scenery of God's creation. I longed to see the crystal blue ocean, white sandy beach, and feel the wind blowing across my face one last time. It wasn't my decision to go to another room, but I wasn't disappointed, because where we ended up was equally beautiful.

This part of the island was just as magnificent with the blue water, white sand, and trees. After being on the island of Anjouan, it was just hard to believe there was such a great difference between the two islands. From the staging, to the physical humidity, to the electricity, and finally the economic difference, God showed me the good, the bad, and the ugly, all in two weeks time. I believe this was to prove to me that I am blessed to live where I do, blessed to have the things I have, and blessed to be able to live a so-called normal life. (Even though I'm not the so called 'normal' person because of my disability.) God proved to me that I *can* make a transformation in other people's lives, not only the disabled, but also I can help other people be open-minded toward their fellow human beings.

When my injured player walked by me, I had to laugh. She had her arm in that same duct taped sling, had a smile on her face, and said she had slept better than she thought. Her arm wasn't hurting as much and she had started moving it some. Praise God. Her entourage, schoolmates and basketball friends, helped carry her bags and were there for her every need.

When it was time to leave, I told Scott to keep in touch, and we traded addresses. I reached over and handed Scott $20 to help him. I also gave $20 to four other people in my group to anonymously give to Scott. About 6:00 P.M. we were taken to the airport for our final destination: home. Just like traveling to the Comoro Islands, I was once again lifted and carried up the airport stairs to the airplane. I was seated at the back of the plane away from my group, but that was okay with me, until something happened. When the plane reached the desired altitude, people were allowed to smoke, and guess where? That's right. They came to the back of the plane with me. I don't smoke, but for a while I was a second-hand-smoker, and I became a pro-smoker with the best of them. Once I almost asked for a cigarette just to be part of the group. I had red eyes, smelled of smoke, and even tasted smoke when I ate! So all I needed was a cigarette to have the full experience, but I declined on that thought.

After a few hours of the flight, we would be making a layover at Yemen – an eighteen-hour layover. When we got to Yemen, we were told by the American embassy to go to our rooms and not to attract attention to ourselves. We were just to relax until it was time to leave.

I went to my room to take a nap and later took a shower because it would be my last chance to clean up before arriving home. We made our way from the third floor where all of our rooms were, to the second floor where the dining room was. I was looking out the window when I noticed that there were cable disks everywhere. I could hear loud music, not music but chants. My understanding is that this chant was from the people praying at different times of the day. It was finally time for us to leave, and the American embassy was notified. It was my understanding that it was a good time for us to leave because Osama bin Laden's people found out we were there. We were not to worry, but to go to the airport and not bring attention to ourselves. This was July 2001, just months before 9/11. God had his hands all over us to provide protection from any harm and give us peace of mind for safety.

When we arrived at the airport, it was kind of strange. There were ten-to-twelve year old children dressed in suits.

They looked like miniature men dressed up, and they were all smoking. They wanted to help carry our bags, so they could earn tips.

We all got on the plane safely and made our way to Germany for a three-hour layover. The funniest thing to me, was finding a McDonalds in the airport. We were eating there like it was our first time, devouring hamburgers and fries. In reality, this McDonalds was a taste of the familiar... proof that home was merely a short distance away.

I was getting tired, but couldn't sleep sitting up. My body was energized and when we were flying over the Atlantic Ocean, and I looked out one side of the plane. It was pitch black, while on the opposite side of the plane it was light. That was an awesome sight. We were in-between the change of darkness and light.

The rest of the flight was tranquil and non-eventful. I sat there getting my second-hand smoke and tried to communicate with the people and have fun. My injured player seemed comfortable, moving her arm with less pain. She had been a silent leader with her courage and bravery.

We arrived in Nashville on the 4th of July. Our family and friends were there to celebrate our return and take us home. Bear was with everyone else. He helped me collect my bags, and we headed to Gallatin. He was asking questions about the trip, but I was tired and non-responsive. When we arrived home, I took a long nap. When I awoke, I was re-energized and ready to tell the rest of my family about my voyage, and what I learned from the other side of the world.

I later found out my injured player didn't break her arm but severely sprained it. She had physical therapy and was as good as new. She didn't miss any games during the basketball season due to her Comoro injury. Thank God.

My trip to Africa was eye opening and uplifting. My faith was reaffirmed as I learned to put my trust in the Lord. I knew that once overseas' all the laws that protect people with disabilities in the United States would no longer apply. It was good for me to surrender to dependence on others to help me get around, up and down stairs, in and out of showers, and other ways that I had previously only allowed family to do for me. God knew I was going on this trip before I did. He prepared the path with the right people for me to be with – "Trust in the Lord with all your heart, and lean not on your own understanding; in all your ways acknowledge Him, and He shall direct your paths" (Proverbs 3:5, 6). He prepared a safe journey so I would be at peace in my mind – "You will keep him in perfect peace, whose mind is stayed on you, because he trusts in you'" (Isaiah 26:3). God provided me the confidence of knowing He will be with me – "In God I have put my trust; I will not be afraid. What can man do to me?" (Psalm 56:11).

Be strong and courageous. Do not be afraid or terrified because of them, for the LORD your God goes with you; he will never leave you nor forsake you."

Deuteronomy 31:6

Chapter Twelve
The Beginning of the End

*Don't ask for a light load, but
rather ask for a strong back.*

Anonymous

THE NEXT FIVE years were good with nothing out of the ordinary happening. My friend Bruce went back to college to get his master's degree. After completion, he decided to work on his Ed. D., a doctorate of education. Several times he approached me or called me, trying to get me on board with him to earn a doctorate degree. I wasn't interested.

In 2006, after our undefeated basketball season, there was a head coaching position open at a nearby high school. I've always wanted to coach at the high school level. After twelve years of experience in teaching and coaching, I applied for the position. While at the middle school level, several awards came my way; teacher of the year, co-coach of the year with Rick, and coach of the year as well. My personal coaching history included involvement in ten championship games. Even though I had great success and enjoyed the teachers I worked with, it was time for a change.

The interview went great, and the principal said he would make his decision by the end of the week. I received a call from the athletic director and was notified that I wasn't getting the job. Even though I had a good interview and it seemed the principal and athletic director enjoyed learning my philosophy of coaching, another coach was hired.

I was angry. I had more experience than the coach they chose, and deserved a chance to prove that I could do the job. Sometimes people suffer from the decisions/choices of others – good or bad. I decided to get my Ed. D. and leave the system.

During the summer, I took my entrance test, filled out my application, and gathered all required papers sending them to Tennessee State University in Nashville. In the fall, an interview took place with the Department Head of Teaching and Learning, as well as a lengthy meeting with a committee. After the interview, I was supposed to be notified the next day, as to whether I had been accepted into the program. On the drive home, the Department Head called me and congratulated me for being accepted. He couldn't wait until the next day to tell me; he was excited for me and I got excited as well. After fifteen years of being out of college, I was off to earn a doctorate in education like Bruce.

Winter was in the air January of 2007, as I started the doctoral program for education. Teaching filled my days and coaching filled the afternoons or evenings, while taking two or three night classes were squeezed into the schedule of my 'never dull' life. In the summer, I was coaching our girls' summer team while taking four doctoral classes, hoping to finish the program as fast as possible. People were telling me that I was taking too much at one time and was going to burn out. My plan was: the more classes I took, the faster I could be done, and friends could start calling me Dr. Coach.

On the first day that teachers were to report to school in August of 2007 I was bitten by a spider on the bottom of my right foot. A few days later, while having a hard time putting on my shoe, I noticed a blister forming on the outside of my heel. That night while in bed, I asked Mom to look at the bottom of my right foot. Something just didn't feel right. She told me there was a huge blister forming on my heel. By the time I realized it was a spider bite, the blister was about the size of a golf ball.

I went to the emergency room, and the doctor examined the blister taking x-rays of my foot. It seemed strange to me to x-ray a blister, knowing I didn't fall to break anything, but he did it anyway. The staff wouldn't listen to me, as I tried to question if it might be a spider bite. The x-ray didn't show anything, so the doctor deduced that I had a pressure sore and sent me home. My instructions were not to force the blister or put pressure on it in any way. After inquiring as to whether or not we should drain the blister, I was rejected and told the fluid was a natural healing medicine the body produces. A few days later, I noticed the blister was about the size of a tennis ball. Later on that night, the blister finally opened up and drained.

About two days later, I noticed the blister had changed to a lot of black tissue. After calling my doctor, he said to get to his office quickly because the black tissue was actually dead tissue. I was sent to the hospital's wound care center, and they proceeded to remove all the dead tissue. It would take months before this wound healed completely. I went once a week to the wound care doctor, and he continued to remove dead tissue and apply medicine and gauzes. They took measurements so it could be determined that new tissue was regenerating.

I was told not to stand on my foot or allow any pressure that would slow down the growth of the new skin. Because of this, I started losing strength in my legs from not standing; I needed someone to help pull up my pants in the morning so I could go to work. I needed someone to help me get into bed at night because I didn't have the strength to get in bed by myself. Going to the bathroom alone, was no longer an option, because I couldn't stand to pivot or transfer. My family never once complained about all the help I needed, but I was losing my strength and independence.

Being paralyzed at the age of nineteen, due to a spinal cord injury, while playing a sand lot football game, was hard to accept. But, twenty-three years of fighting and working hard to gain and maintain strength to become independent, was more difficult the second time. The constant need to ask someone to assist me got harder and harder. It felt degrading to me.

Depression visited me once again, causing me to feel like a helpless baby.

Mom would come to the house early in the morning after she was finished throwing her newspapers. She would help get my pants up while putting my socks and shoes on. I knew she was tired from being up all night sorting, rolling, and delivering her newspapers. It was making me feel bad knowing she was so tired, and then she had the burden of helping me, rather than going home and getting some sleep.

She always cared more for her children than taking care of herself. Even while going through cancer treatment in having surgery to remove part of her right lung, she was still thinking of her children. She never complained, but my mind dwelled on her surgery when she was helping me get my pants up. I was wondering if somehow I was hurting her right side, but she never indicated about being in pain.

Mom came every day to make sure that I was correctly dressed so I could be successful as a teacher and a coach. Because I couldn't stand up, she placed a sliding board under me, so I could get into my car to drive to work. I knew my mother was proud of me, knowing I was making a difference in my students' lives. When I got to school, I would call someone from inside the building to help me get out of the car, allowing me to be ready to teach.

When school was over, I needed someone to help me into my car again so I could go to my wound care doctor, to my night classes or go home. If I had a class that night, I would go to the university and get a parking place. I sat there until I saw someone who might be strong enough to help me out of my car. Being mindful that I am a large man, I was always hopeful they wouldn't hurt themselves, while helping me get to class. Amazingly, no one I asked to help ever said, "No. I won't help" or simply just walked away. Everybody I asked was glad to help, and considered it a ministry – a blessing for them to be assisting me. After class was over, typically someone would follow me to my car and help me get in, so I could go home.

My two brothers, Bear and Andy, made sure that I got into bed so I wouldn't have to stay up all night. They also made sure that I was able to get to the toilet safely without struggling. Getting out of bed was no problem, because the bed was higher than the wheelchair, but the bed height did pose a problem, making it nearly impossible for me to get *into bed* without assistance. Bear and Andy alternated days of the week, making sure I was able to get into bed.

In an effort to free my family from my personal care, I called my insurance company in the summer of 2008. Might someone be available to come to my home for fifteen minutes each morning and evening? I just needed help getting into bed and putting on my clothes. I was seeking relief for my family members and wondered what help they could provide me?

The insurance company told me that I'd have to quit my job, sell my house and move into a nursing home to get that kind of help.

I said, "You mean I have to lose everything that I worked so hard for, just to receive a total of thirty minutes of assistance a day?"

Their response was, "Yes. That's how the law is setup." I replied with, "That law sucks." Then I hung up.

> *The LORD God said, "It is not good for the man to be alone. I will make a helper suitable for him."*
>
> *Genesis 2:18*

Chapter Thirteen

Good Bye, Andy

When you get to the end of your rope, tie a knot and hang on.

Franklin D. Roosevelt

It was a cold December in 2007. Andy was put into the hospital and it was discovered that his liver enzymes were all out of whack, because of all the alcohol he had consumed over the years. (Andy had started drinking in his early teens by sneaking around with friends his age.) He was told he had a hernia and a bleeding ulcer. They cautioned to be careful how he strained and most importantly, not to pick up anything heavy. He had damaged his liver, but it was not yet to the stage of cirrhosis of the liver. If he quit drinking, his body still had time to heal his liver. The doctor also told Andy that if he continued drinking as he had done for years, he had a ten percent chance of living five more years. When Andy got out of the hospital, he was like most other alcoholics, he tried to quit drinking cold turkey, and like most alcoholics, he didn't do well. He tried his best for two weeks not to drink, but before he knew it he was slowly back to where he began. He drank as much as he had before, I really felt he had slowed down, but he didn't stop.

On October 22, 2008, Andy and my mother came to help me into bed that night. I noticed Andy was very pale, and he didn't seem to have a lot of energy. We all three talked for a little while. Andy had been sick for over a year and a half. That night, even though Andy was pale and seemed tired, he still helped me into bed. He never once complained about helping me, even though it was obvious he wasn't feeling good. Later on that night, October 23, 2008, Mom called about three o'clock in the morning telling me we were about to lose Andy. Thirty minutes later, Mom called back and said that the ambulance got there and couldn't do anything to revive him. I felt partially responsible for Andy losing his life that night because I was not able to get into bed by myself.

To top everything else off, the police treated my mother as if she had killed Andy. She was not allowed to go into the room where he was, nor was she allowed to go to her neighbor for comfort, and the final straw occurred when she was not allowed to call her boss to explain why she couldn't finish her paper route. The officers questioned her as if she were a suspect in his murder. My mother told the police that my brother had a drinking problem and other health issues, but they wouldn't listen to her. Instead, they interrogated her in her own home, asking ridiculous questions. Did she and Andy have an argument early in the day? When was the last time she had seen him alive? What was he like when she went to work? Did she know anyone that he may have had an argument with earlier in the day? Apparently, she didn't answer their questions like they wanted, so she was put into the police car to fill out papers downtown. A mother who had just lost her child was treated like she was an ax murderer.

I got out of bed about five o'clock in the morning so that I could call administrators to let them know that I would not be in, due to the death of my brother. After arriving at my mother's house about 6:30 in the morning; she began telling me how she had been treated by the police. My temperature flared and I drove to the police station demanding to speak to the supervisor in charge. I explained to him how the officers treated my mother, *as if she had killed my brother.* They had no compassion, only a cocky attitude.

He offered a flimsy explanation that they might have been young people, rookies, still in training at the site. My reply was if that was true, then these rookies needed to shut their mouths and learn from the veterans who should have been in charge. Those police were representing him, and they didn't do a good job of it.

By this time, Mom had come up to the police station, and she got to talk with the police supervisor that's when the "final slap in the face" was complete. She asked for Andy's belongings, wanting his most recent picture, his driver's license, and any other personal items they might have. The police supervisor got on the computer and informed my mother and me that they didn't have his belongings. He said that the ambulance service should have them. My mother responded that she had been told by the ambulance service, that it was the responsibility of the police to gather materials so they could verify who the body was. He again said the police didn't have the belongings, and then suggested we check with the funeral director. My mother's friend who was the funeral director gave the same answer as the ambulance service, saying it was the police's responsibility to get that material. The police supervisor again confirmed there was no report showing they had the belongings.

This meant one of three things must have taken place that night: first, the police did not do their job because they were focused on finding a murderer; second, neglect took place, resulting in a total disregard for my brother's belongings; and third, they thought my brother and mother were nothing more than poor white trash because they lived in a mobile home. As I see it, they felt my brother and mother didn't deserve their best attention in preserving any memories… resulting in a total lack of respect for my family. Andy died two weeks before his thirty-eighth birthday, nearly two years from the time the doctors warned him about continuing to drink. Andy didn't make it to those five years. We never found his belongings.

My heart was heavy and my mind could not release the feeling that I was responsible for Andy being dead. Why didn't I insist that he no longer lift me, after the doctor told him not to pick up anything heavy? My mother, brother Tim, and others told me that I shouldn't view Andy's death as anything but his personal sacrifice of love. He wanted to give his time, strength, and courage for my personal well-being. Andy knew what the doctors told him, but he wanted to help me so I would be comfortable and rested, totally prepared for teaching the next day. They assured me that Andy would be honored and grateful knowing he made things easier for me. In the New International Version, John 15:13 explains it like this, "Greater love has no one than this, that he lay down his life for his friends."

I requested the following story be told at Andy's Memorial Service.

Having pulled up in my mother's driveway, I saw Andy finishing a man's vehicle that had needed repaired. The man asked Andy how much he owed him and tried to pay him, but Andy kept saying the man owed him nothing and wouldn't take any money. The man shook Andy's hand and went about his business. I pulled up to Andy and said, "Andy, how are you making money if you give your time and labor away free to your customers?"

Andy replied, "He has cancer, and this is one way I can help him."

After that day, I decided to stay out of Andy's business because he knew how to operate his business better than I did. Andy, like all of us, had his own problems and his own personal demons. Andy's demon was alcohol. Even though he drank, he would get up and go to work, always finding ways to help his fellow man without thinking about himself.

My feeling that I was responsible for Andy's death became all-consuming and on January 22, 2009, I went to my principal to ask for a medical leave from school. It was my intention to take off the rest of January and all of February for physical therapy, to help gain strength and get back some of the independence I had lost. I had become severely depressed feeling like a burden to people, and of course, still feeling partially responsible for the death of Andy. The principal filled out papers and signed them so I could take a medical leave and come back to school at the beginning of March to finish the school year.

The next day, I met with a preacher after school, at the principal's suggestion, due to my depression and her fear that I might try to "do something" to myself. I counseled with the pastor and two other members of the church for nearly two hours. I confided in them about how hard life seemed for the last year and a half. My sorrow was compounded by daily physical pain for nearly twenty-six years. I admitted my embarrassment in the morning, needing someone to help dress me by pulling up my pants, so I could go to work. Then I shared the added sadness of needing help to get into bed at night, because I couldn't do it anymore. My overwhelming sorrow was that I was a burden on my family, and added the final "whammy"… I felt partially responsible for my brother's death.

Honestly, I know I didn't harm or kill my brother, I had been in a deep depression for about a year before his death, but my brother's death exacerbated my depression. Since I had been so depressed, the only thing I could think of was if I hadn't become so weak and helpless, I could have gotten into bed by myself, and Andy would still be here today. Being in such a long state of depression can totally fog anyone's mind and make them believe that they are responsible for all bad things. Every time someone helped pull my pants up, helped with my personal hygiene, or helped me get into bed, all I could think about was how much easier life would be for the people around me if I were not there.

The preacher encouraged me and said that people loved me and wanted to help. He said he had known for a long time now that I was hurting and needed help, but he didn't know what my needs were and how to help. I told him that people had helped me for long enough and that I couldn't help anybody or have an impact on anybody.

He told me that I had inspired numerous people by my teaching, coaching, and overcoming adversities. He shared I had impacted so many people's lives because I was not a quitter. He added, my accomplishments were a blessing to others.

I kept insisting my biggest concern was the toll my personal care was taking on my family. My perception was, I was taking more than I could give, and that wasn't right. They pressed me for a verbal commitment that I would not "do anything" to myself and we decided it was time to go.

While leaving the school building, I noticed that basketball practice for the girls was almost over. I didn't want to go through the gym to get into my van. The preacher, the other two people, and the boys' basketball coach didn't want me to go through there either. Not that they told me that, but they kept me in the hallway outside of the gym telling me stories to occupy my time until the team left.

The preacher told me about how he got into his first college basketball game. The boys' basketball coach was telling some story about the time he was teaching and coaching in Kentucky. All of this took about fifteen minutes for the girls to get out of the gym to be picked up. They were buying time to keep me there, I didn't notice, but in hindsight it is now clear.

Then all of the sudden, two sheriffs came into the building and questioned me about what was going on. Apparently, the sheriff's office had been contacted by the principal, who didn't feel comfortable letting me go home. She advised the assistant principal to contact the sheriff to take me to the hospital for an evaluation. This didn't set well with me.

One of the officers asked me what was going on. I replied that I was trying to leave, and these people would not let me go. While he was talking to me, his partner was standing beside me with his hand on his pepper spray and the other hand rattling the handcuffs. He stood there with this 'Sgt. Carter look', his sheriff's hat pulled down just above his eyebrows, just staring at me. He never said a word. The other officer raised his voice at me and spoke in a demanding way.

If they really thought that I was going to do something to myself, maybe this behavior wasn't the way to encourage me not to attempt anything. These two guys were trying to get some control over the situation, but the way they were acting just caused more tension.

The situation escalated out of control while I was yelling at the preacher and the others, the sheriffs, and the boys' basketball coach. I screamed at the preacher that I had spoken to him in a confidential manner; that I had opened up to him because I was hurting and asked if this was his way of helping. I thought that if I confided in him, then he wasn't supposed to talk or tell anyone about it. He had broken confidentiality and replied they loved me too much to allow me to do anything to myself.

I told the sheriff that there was no law that says suicide is against the law. He replied that if I was harmful to myself or to someone else, then they could stop me. I again said there was no law specifying that suicide is illegal. The officer wanted to know what they could do help me. I looked at him and said he and Sgt. Carter could leave so I could go home.

He then told me that he had the right to have me committed to the hospital for evaluation. He felt that I was harmful to myself and that I needed to go for a psychological evaluation. I told him I wasn't going, and he had no right to force me. He let me know that I was going, even if he had to put me on the floor, handcuff me, and force me to go.

This answer was wrong, and he could not force me to go. He continued that it was in his right and again stressed that he would put me out of my wheelchair and handcuff me to make me go.

He thought himself such a big man – to threaten a guy in a wheelchair. It must have made him feel good to bully a man who can barely push himself around. He just stood there and glared at me.

I again released my anger on the pastor and the others. They continued to respond that they loved me too much to let me do anything to myself. It occurred to me, if this is love, no wonder

I'm a single man. My former friend, the basketball coach was squatting down on the floor with his head on his knees. I asked him if he was part of this conspiracy. He sheepishly put his head up and shook his head no. Only a week earlier, he had told me that I was his best friend at school. I was so disappointed in him, blurting out, "If this is the way you treat your best friend, I don't need a friend like you!" He was caught in what's called, 'friendly fire.' In retrospect, I don't believe he knew this was going to take place.

Things quieted down for a while, and I was looking out the front door. We were waiting for the ambulance. Then about that time one of the assistant principals came in. I asked him, "Are you part of this conspiracy?"

He said, "Yes, sir" to me. I thanked him for his honesty. I asked him if he knew that I went to the principal and asked for a medical leave. He said, "Yes."

I said, "Tell her I don't need to take a medical leave anymore, tell her that I quit." He wanted to know why I was going to quit, when I had never quit before. He then took me into the guidance counselor's office, away from everyone, and talked to me.

The ambulance came and took me off to the hospital for an evaluation. The people who picked me up were nice and respectful. The guy in the back of the ambulance was talking with me, keeping me calm. He was better than the others, explaining the procedure to me so I would know what to expect at the hospital.

Early in his life, he also had wanted to end it all – but couldn't do it because of his children. After seeking professional help, he admitted to getting past his depression. He was encouraging to me instead of bullying and making false statements, like – we love you too much...

After an hour in the emergency room, a doctor came in and talked with me. He requested I confide in a psychologist. By then, I had cooled off and decided to play the game. I reassured everyone that, yes, I was depressed, but I wouldn't try to kill myself because that was a selfish act. It wasn't right that someone else would have to clean up my mess after suicide. I let them know I had thought about it when I first got in a wheelchair, but I couldn't do it. I was released by the doctors that same night and went home.

> *Accept the one whose faith is weak, without quarreling over disputable matters.*
> *Romans 14:1*

Chapter Fourteen
Strike Three – You're Not Out

*Accept challenges, so that you may
feel the exhilaration of victory.*

George S. Patton

I LIKED TO WATCH the Cubs play especially when it was time for Harry Carey to sing the seventh inning stretch, "Take me out to the ballgame." The last line of the song says, "For it's one… two… three strikes you're out at the old ballgame." In baseball, when the third strike happens, the batter is out and the next batter comes to the plate, the inning ends allowing the other team to come in and hit, or the game is over.

Sometimes the catcher misses or mishandles the third strike pitched, allowing the hitter to reach first base. Because of this miscue, the team has another chance at the plate to potentially add more runs and to continue the game. Life is the same. There are situations that allow us to continue – when we thought life was not worth living any longer. We sometimes give up when life gets tough, and we think we can't handle anymore of what life has given to us. We were never promised a rose garden, but instead we sometimes receive lemons that give us a sour taste of life in our mouth. The old saying about Murphy's Law, if anything can go wrong it will, is especially true in any part of life. You learn the law as you get older and have more experience as you graduate from the school of life.

Strike One

The physical pain of wheelchair confinement compounded by the death of my brother was playing games with my head. I decided it was time to end the suffering. On Friday, January 30, 2009, my suicide plan was put into action. I would withdraw all my money and close my accounts, leaving a note for my mother and Bear directing them to the money hidden in the house.

But the bank didn't have enough money to give me since it was Friday, payday. They needed to make sure there was money for people cashing their checks. I could close my accounts and pick up the money on Wednesday of the next week. I informed them I wouldn't be here next Wednesday and needed my money today. The bank finally let me withdraw $2,000. I got a form for my mother to sign so she would be on my account as a joint owner, allowing her to get the money later.

On the way home, I stopped at Wal-Mart to buy brown legal envelopes to put the money in and purchased two boxes of Sudafed. Here in Tennessee a law had been passed that anyone who buys Sudafed had to provide identification and sign a form because people were getting this medication to use as an ingredient to make meth. The Sudafed box directs people to take no more than two tablets every six hours, due to drowsiness. It states no more than four doses should be taken in a twenty-four hour period – that's eight pills in one day. It warns not to operate heavy machinery because of drowsiness.

The next day, Saturday, January 31, 2009, I started emptying the packs of Sudafed. I needed a generic Last Will Testament form from online so I could leave my family everything. I typed my suicide letter on the computer. This is the actual letter:

Mom and Bear,

I love you so much. I wouldn't have been successful in life without you two and Andy. Both of you have been great as a family. All of you have sacrificed so much for me. Mom, you gave of yourself more than anybody could ask for. Mom, do something for yourself – think about you some. Get your eyes checked. Bear, find a great wife – you have so much to offer. Please don't take this too hard but it is the best. Just think no more physical pain, no more emotional pain, and no more mental pain. Now I can provide you something. I believe I'm in heaven even though this happened. The Bible tells us that Jesus paid for our sins. That means He paid for our sins from the beginning of our lives to the end. People say that this act of death means someone must be mentally ill. The Bible says God takes care of these types of people. And I asked for forgiveness before.

Mom, you can do whatever is best with the house. You can move in and put a fence around the house for the dogs. They can live under the screened porch. Or it might be better at your house because you have Betty, Andy, Ronnie, Ben, and Elizabeth as friends, neighbors, and support. If you sell the house, call Margret to sell 230 – ****. I withdrew $2,000 from checking to help you in case my accounts get frozen. There is a paper that you need to sign and put your Social Security number on as being my joint account. Friday's date, January 30, 2009 is already on it. You'll need to sign it in front of the papers. Below are my accounts where you can get more money. I don't think there is anything else.

Debit Card Pin Number **** – go to Walgreens and the ATM is free – no service charge to remove money.

US Financial Life – look in the brown divider under the desk.

Make sure you tell them Andy is deceased and send them a copy of his death certificate so Bear and you can split that money.
Roth 401

One More Play

Cash it in
503B
Cash it in

I have a death benefit because of teaching. Call the School Board of Education. Cash it in – find out where my retirement goes, make sure it comes to you.

Bear, I have my income tax coming to your checking account. A little over $3,000 – watch for it in about two weeks.

I've signed the title to the van. You can get Tennessee Mobility to sell it for you or pass it back to the church so they can find someone that can use it. Do whatever you think best.

Have Bruce call Dr. Pangle to tell him I won't be finishing the doctoral program. Tell Bruce to get all my college books and sell at TSU. Some are on the desk and others are in Wuzz's closet.

You know I've never really been happy in a wheelchair. Yes, there were a lot of good times but over all I never liked it. The best part of being disabled was knowing that I had a family that sacrificed themselves to make sure I was comfortable and successful.

I love both of you. If we could handpick our families – this one is the one for me. I'll see you in heaven.

James

After writing my good-bye letter to the family, I put it in an envelope along with my debit card, credit cards, and the $2,000 I withdrew from the bank the day before. I went online searching for a Last Will and Testament form. Since I had never done this before, I didn't want my soon-to-be inheritance to go to a probate court and some stranger decide what happened to my materials. This way I knew my family would do the right thing with their new possessions.

Next, I needed to do one more thing. I took both packs of Sudafed and opened all of the tiny containers that held the pills. I released the medication from the restriction of the package with the expectation that these capsules would soon relieve me from the bondage of pain. The pain I wanted to be released from was not only physical but also mental and spiritual. Being worn down from the physical pain of being paralyzed was a factor, but also mentally, I was drained from trying to hide my depression and tired putting on a front for everyone to see. It was harder and harder spiritually, satan being the 'great accuser' constantly reminded me that I was good for nothing. The voices shouted that I was responsible for Andy's death, and I would never get any better. Deep into my heart, I knew suicide wasn't the answer to the problem. However, the lure of releasing myself from pain, setting my family free from my

One More Play

daily care and dependence, seemed too tantalizing to ignore. I decided to take the next step...

I took the envelope with all of my personal affairs, to the post office so Mom would have everything by Monday. While I was out, I took the empty medication wrappers and boxes, dropping them in a trash can miles away. I knew I was killing myself, but I didn't want anyone to know how I died by walking in and seeing the evidence. On my way home, I was praying to God to forgive me for my sins. After all, Mom did always say there was only one unforgivable sin: suicide.

I got home and wrote e-mails to my friends, thanking them for being my friends and all they had done for me. I sent these e-mails to their work, so they wouldn't know what I was doing until it was too late. They wouldn't get the e-mails until Monday, and I would be dead and gone. I sent a special friend one of the crosses with the Lord's Prayer on it. About 7 P.M., I took all the capsules, forty-eight of them, in less than three minutes. The package said not to take more than six pills in a twenty-four-hour period. I took eight times the required limit of medicine, and got out of my wheelchair so I could lie on the bedroom floor to die. That way, if I needed help, it would be impossible to call someone to rescue me.

I started praying again for God to forgive me for what I was doing. As I was praying, I noticed a sense of relief, a sense of peace, knowing that I would no longer hurt or be in pain from anything again. Mom said that suicide is the unforgivable sin because when you are dead you can't ask for forgiveness, but, thanks to the Baptists, once saved – always saved. I was taught that when Jesus was crucified, his blood covered all my sins before and after my life. I was in peace knowing I would no longer be suffering here on Earth, and would be in Heaven due to Jesus' blood and his forgiveness.

I lay on the floor for the next four and a half hours, and all I got was a headache that caused my muscles to spasm. I wasn't drowsy, not even tired enough to go to sleep. Bear would soon be coming over to watch Saturday Night Live and help me into bed. I needed to come up with an excuse for being on the floor. When he arrived, I spun this tale... I told him I was cleaning my glasses and dropped them. While I was trying to pick up my glasses, I lost my balance and fell to the ground. Bear tried to get me off the floor so I could go to bed, but he couldn't lift me, and of course, I couldn't help. We had to call the paramedics to get me into bed. I was praying that night while in bed that the overdose of medicine would take effect and I would die overnight.

Strike Two

Super Bowl Sunday was the next day. I awoke around 9 A.M. having had the best night's sleep in a long time! I lay in bed thinking about what I had tried and what I was going to do next. Instead of being grateful and thankful to the Lord for sparing my life, I still felt depressed. I knew my situation hadn't and wouldn't change, so there was no need to try to do anything but try killing myself again.

As I tried to get out of bed, my limbs tremored violently and unexpectedly. I guess all the medicine taken was causing my muscles to shake uncontrollably, and my muscles were weaker than usual. I was trying to get out of bed, but was getting nervous that I would be too weak to transfer to my wheelchair. As I was taking the risk, Bear came by before going to work and held the wheelchair so I could get in it.

Now that Bear had left, I needed to figure out what to do. I called CVS and told them I needed something for insomnia. Telling them I hadn't slept well for the last three nights, I needed something to help me sleep. The pharmacist suggested Benadryl. I went to Wal-Mart again to buy Benadryl. All I had was six dollars. I had already mailed my credit cards and debit card along with all the money to my mother. So, one pack of twenty-four capsules of Benadryl was all I could afford. Good grief, you'd think when a man is trying to kill himself he could afford to do it right!

I got home with the box and started emptying the individual containers like I did before with the Sudafed. As I was working hard and vigorously, Mom came in the house to visit. While we were talking, I was covering up the pills so she wouldn't figure out what I was doing to question me. She talked about work, the weather, whatever was in the news, and of course, me. Even though I tried to put on a front for her and everyone else, she saw through it. She let me know that I shouldn't feel bad about Andy dying, but I needed to be glad he wanted to help and loved me. But I was so depressed, I heard what she said but *failed to listen.* I was focused on getting her out of the house so I could try once again to end my life.

When Mom left, I continued with my final mission of opening and emptying the packages of Benadryl. The drugs I had already taken made my fingers weaker than normal which made the chore even harder. After getting all twenty-four pills out of the packages, I started to gather the empty box and the receipt, to drive down the road and dispose of the garbage. Again, hoping to remove any immediate trace of what caused my death. When I got home, my cat Wuzz, jumped on my lap and I petted him as I took all the pills at one time. Like the night before, I wasn't scared or fearful while taking the overdose because I knew all would be over. With the cocktail of Benadryl and Sudafed, there was so much dope in me; chances were I would sleep forever. This time I didn't get on the floor, just in case something went wrong – if I didn't die. That way I wouldn't get Bear suspicious of what was going on. I put my head on my desk and prayed to God to forgive me for what I was doing and ask Him to protect and bless Mom and Bear.

As I laid my head down, I had the Super Bowl pregame show turned on, but I have no memory of it or the game. With the overdose of pills, I fell asleep all right, but only enough to miss all of the game before waking up about 9 P.M. There was one thing that I do remember that day. My mother called during the game, but I don't recall the content of the conversation, except for one thing. I was slurring my words and talking slowly. My mother asked me what was wrong with my voice, and I told her I was tired and had cotton-mouth. I needed to get some water and take a nap. I was worried she would come over and find me dead. Thankfully, she didn't come over. Bear showed up for his usual nightly "lifting my brother" and I slept optimistic I would accomplish my death in the night.

Strike Three – You're Not Out

It was Monday morning, February 2, 2009, and I was still here. Another good night's rest, with all that medication in me, I'm shocked to be alive. I don't remember much of anything from yesterday except for the phone conversation with Mom. Well, not the conversation but her asking what was wrong. I barely recall that I was tired and my mouth was dry. But other than that, I don't remember yesterday.

I got out of bed about 7:30 A.M. with Mom holding my chair, because my muscles were reacting more violently than yesterday. The phone began ringing; I had five phone calls in a span of three minutes. People were reading the e-mails I had sent from Saturday night. They wanted to know what was going on. I put on a front with my mother there and with the people on the phone. Explaining, I was writing to let everyone know I loved them and was thanking them for all they had done for me. It seemed I convinced them they were reading too much into the situation... buying me more time. The phone calls stopped. Then I remembered I had sent Mom an envelope with all of my suicide material. I had to do something quick because I wouldn't be able to stop the mail, and soon more phone calls would be coming.

After Mom helped me get dressed, we talked awhile and then she left. I gave her time to leave and time to make sure she wasn't coming back. Then I decided to try again to kill myself. This time with no money, debit or credit cards, I decided to get in my van and inhale exhaust fumes until I was asphyxiated.

I got into my van and shut the door to the garage. I started the van and was about to get out of my wheelchair when I thought of something. Turning off the engine, I went back into the house to find my cats Wuzz and Spud, not wanting them to die from the carbon monoxide; I put them outside for safety.

After returning to the van, I noticed the clock said 9 A.M. I started the van. Next, I parked my wheelchair in the back of the van and transferred to the floor. This way, if I started feeling bad, getting nauseated, I wouldn't be able to leave the garage and call for help. I lay on the van floor listening to the radio while trying to go to sleep. I was inhaling the sweet tasting fumes as fast as possible. It seemed to take a long time filling the garage and the van. I just kept listening to the radio while breathing in this toxic odor.

It was after 11 A.M. when I noticed the van starting to choke out. I assumed it was from the carbon monoxide taking the place of oxygen. There must be a sensory chip that knows there is a lack of oxygen, and after about ten minutes of the van's trying to choke out, the van stopped running. I remember coughing, getting light-headed, and telling myself, "Great, I'm now going to live and have brain damage." So I gasped harder and faster to take in the gas before it left the garage. I don't remember passing out, but I must have.

Around 1 P.M. my neighbor, Terry came to visit me. He found me lying on the van floor with my body fighting for oxygen. He could see my stomach, my diaphragm, vigorously working to get fresh oxygen. There was a verse that reminded him about God's breath of life. Genesis 2:7, "Then the LORD God formed a man from the dust of the ground and breathed into his nostrils the breath of life, and the man became a living being." Terry didn't know CPR, so he started slapping me on the face, trying to get me to regain consciousness, but that didn't work... so he called 911.

The paramedics arrived and gave me oxygen. I don't know everything that was done, but I woke up with IV's started, an oxygen mask on, my blood pressure being taken, and questions were being asked. I was alive again and there was no way out of my pain and suffering. I started crying knowing I would continue being a burden to my family and apparently my attempt to kill myself was feudal. This wasn't fair. People were quick to say, "Keep trying to live; things will get better. Don't give up; stay strong." Things didn't get better, they got worse. I had questions of my own: Where are all of these people when I need help putting on my shoes and socks? Where are you when my body is too heavy to manipulate on and off the toilet? When I am desperate to take a shower and have no one to assist me, how can I ever think things will get better? How am I supposed to maintain my independence, with these looming physical needs? All of these thoughts festered in my mind making me bitter toward life and people.

I was taken to the hospital for medical evaluation and to be stabilized. Mom and Bear came in wondering what happened. I admitted to them, I was trying to kill myself. The look on their faces made me hurt even more. Then I was placed in a hyperbaric chamber or a decompression chamber for oxygen therapy. This lasted for three to four hours, removing the carbon monoxide from my body, forcing oxygen in its place. While I was in the chamber, the nurses noticed I had a burn. It was on my right hip and outer right leg. I must have gotten burned while lying on the van floor. Heat apparently came up from the exhaust and heated the floor. Now, not only was I alive, but also I had a burn to deal with.

I was in the critical care unit for about a week and of course, was on suicide watch. A psychiatrist came in twice a day and asked me how I felt and if I wanted to talk about what happened. I explained about being a burden, losing independence and Andy's death for which I felt partially responsible, leading me to make the decision to end it all. I was certain that I was going to a psych hospital for a mental evaluation, but that didn't happen. The doctor and the psychiatrist reviewed my situation and decided that I needed physical therapy to gain strength and to learn different ways of keeping my independence.

The rehabilitation floor of the hospital became my new home. The therapists there were motivating, positive, encouraging, and supportive to me. They helped me relearn dressing myself in bed. They gave multiple ideas on how to transfer in and out of bed, on and off the toilet, and ways to build strength in my upper body. The main thing that amazed me was the therapists desire to help me get better. They made me believe that life was worthwhile – even better than I could imagine! It was apparent this was their calling, the reason they do what they do – to help others get better so they can enjoy life to the fullest.

For seven long weeks, I called the hospital home... meeting with a psychologist weekly, became very beneficial. He suggested I join Toastmasters. Learning to tell my story through Toastmasters has convinced me that I am able to help others who are suffering.

The psychologist gave me homework while in the hospital. He had me read, a book entitled *Man's Search for Meaning*, by Viktor Frankl. This book had a major impact on my life. Each day, I was assigned a chapter to read, then morning discussions would follow. The book records Dr. Frankl's experiences in a concentration camp. He describes the fear of being captured, wondering whether he would live or die, weight loss from excessive labor and eating only two pieces of bread a day. Life inside the camp was unbearable, but people held captive continually reminded each other to consider their purpose for living. Even though Dr. Frankl lost his wife during that time, he determined his purpose for living was to continue his research when he was freed. No matter the tragedies, suffering, or devastations, we must believe that life always has meaning. Meaning can be discovered through family, friends, or God... no matter the situation, it is imperative to find your purpose in life. So I ask you, the reader: What provides your meaning – purpose in life? Whether it's your spouse, children, working for your next vacation, or helping others, I challenge you to discover your purpose for living.

After reading Dr. Frankl's book, my perspective changed. Living life to the fullest for me will require some assistance. God has provided me with a family that graciously supports me. To deny their help is to slap God in the face. My purpose involves my family. We are "one" in life... loving, giving, sharing... equal participants in life together. With laughter, sorrow, and tears – we jointly support one another.

The Psychologist helped me to see how blessed I am. I am not just a "taker." My attitude and gratitude are all contributions I can make to better each of my family's lives. My purpose is to support and encourage others with disabilities. Also, to raise the awareness of "normal" people, helping them to see that all individuals have worth. The body is merely a casement of man. What is most important is the soul of the person. God creates all people with uniqueness. There is value in going beyond judgment to acceptance and love. I want to be a "builder of men" not one who destroys those in my path. You too, can determine what you will do with the power of your "purpose."

> *Blessed is the man who perseveres under trial, because when he has stood the test, he will receive the crown of life that God has promised to those who love him.*
>
> *James 1:12*

Chapter Fifteen
There's No Need To Fear – Ricardo Is Here

Those who dream by night in the dusty recesses of their minds wake in the day to find that all was vanity; but the dreamers of the day are dangerous men, for they may act their dream with open eyes, and make it possible.

T. E. Lawrence (Lawrence of Arabia)

ONE SATURDAY MORNING, about a year before my suicide attempt, I was transferring out of bed to my wheelchair when my chair rolled out from under me. Falling to the floor like a sack of potatoes, I was unable to get to the phone. While lying on the floor, wondering how long I would be there before anyone missed me, I started cussing and crying. It was then I started planning my big adventure. It was time to drag myself from my bedroom to the living room to call for help. I could only drag myself one to three inches at any given time. After pulling with my arms and pushing with my legs, it took a burst of energy to make that one-inch move. I rested ten to fifteen minutes before exerting myself again. The twenty-five foot trip took me two and a half hours. After receiving cuts and scratches on my face, legs, and arms as proof of my efforts, I was finally able to call EMTs for assistance.

On the following Monday, I talked with someone about what happened that weekend. She told me she had a niece who trains dogs for the blind, and she would see what could be done for me. Later that week, she gave me information about the company, Canine Companion for Independence, an organization that trains dogs to help individuals with disabilities to sustain their independence. The canine companion can pick up items on the floor, open and close drawers and doors, turn lights on and off, but what I heard loudly was that they could bring a phone when needed.

I got on the website and called CCI to start the process of receiving a dog. The closest CCI is in Orlando, Florida; it represents the Southeastern Region of the United States. After talking with one of the organization program managers, she told me there were four steps to the process. CCI sent a package of papers to fill out, eight pages of information were required and that was only the beginning. I rumbled, grumbled and reluctantly filled out the papers. At least this part of the process was done and put in the mail. When completing the first step, I was wondering if this was worth it.

Step two was put into action, after receiving a phone call from CCI. A phone interview which lasted thirty to forty-

One More Play

five minutes was my next assignment. The following week came and CCI called. The phone interviewer asked the same questions that were on the application. There was one question I remember: Did I have a preference in the color, sex, or breed in the dog? I wanted a mix between a collie and a pit-bull dog. That way it could protect me by ripping someone's arm off, and it could go get help. We laughed. I didn't care about the kind of dog as long as it was a "chick magnet."

A letter from CCI stated I had passed the phone interview, and it was time for the third part of the process. Another package of papers arrived. They wanted my biography, pictures of my house and land, and papers for my doctor to fill out. Papers were retrieved from my doctor, information was completed and off to Florida – they were sent! Three out of four steps were completed. Unfortunately, this news didn't lift my spirits. As time went by, my depression increased. I kept thinking the same thoughts: about losing independence, a burden to my family and being partly responsible for the cause of my brother's death. I had lost all hopes of life. I didn't see my circumstances changing for the better.

After three weeks in the hospital from attempting suicide, I had my mother and Bear bring my mail so they wouldn't have to pay my bills, and I could read other mail as well. The last week in the hospital, I came across a letter from the Canine Companion for Independence.

The letter stated that CCI had been trying to get in contact with me by phone and email. They needed to know if I was still interested in a canine companion. If still interested, I needed to complete the final step in the process, a personal interview.

They wanted me to drive twelve to thirteen hours to have a three hour interview. At this point, I wasn't sure if this is what I wanted.

My family encouraged me to go to Orlando and complete the process. Bear went with me. At the interview, I got to work with a few dogs to see if they could and would obey my commands. They needed to see if the dogs understood me vocally and if I could perform corrections properly. The atmosphere at CCI was unbelievable. It was not only fun but also positive.

When the personal interview was completed, a team of people got together to discuss if they could train a dog to assist my needs. They came back with a positive answer. They could help me with a canine, and they were confident they would have a dog. No not a dog, but a *canine companion*, soon.

A few months went by, and finally the phone call came. CCI had several dogs for me to work with and would determine the best fit for the dog and me. Eight other families were getting a companion dog along with me. We spent two weeks being trained how to give commands, make corrections, learn grooming, and how to handle our canine in public. After the first four days of working with several dogs, CCI decided Ricardo was the best fit for me.

Ricardo was bred and born in the CCI program in California. When it was time for Ricardo's mother to give birth, CCI used the alphabet system. They were on the letter "R" so all puppies from this litter had to have the letter "R" in the beginning of their name. Then Ricardo appeared, a black lab, he stood tall compared to the other puppies. He had confidence that seemed to ooze out of him from the beginning. Ricardo soon demonstrated the energy of Underdog; he would be like Superman – he was faster than a speeding bullet, he fought crime like Batman, and he had Spiderman powers. Maybe I'm exaggerating and Ricardo is the same as the other puppies, but to me, he would be the answer to my prayers.

When it was time, (*How would Bob Barker put it?*) to neuter Ricardo, he also received a tattoo. On his right ear, he has the numbers 08277. Ricardo was born in the year of '08 and he was the 277th puppy born in CCI's facility that year. When he was eight weeks old, Ricardo was sent to Mississippi to be puppy raised. He spent eighteen months learning commands, such as sit, stand, roll, and commands to know when it was time to toilet or eat. Ricardo is trained not to bark without command, and he learned how to dress himself, putting on his vest, collar, and leash. During the puppy raising-phase, the puppies learn valuable commands and public etiquette that will help them become successful as service canines. Ricardo is familiar with the clanking of bars because he "did time" – or was *puppy-raised* in one of Mississippi's correctional facilities.

After eighteen months of puppy-raising, it was time for Ricardo to receive his final training. He was placed at Orlando, Florida's CCI boot camp for canines. Ricardo learned to retrieve items, hold the items, give the item to the person or drop the item when commanded. He was taught special commands that would make him beneficial to me.

After two weeks of training was completed, Ricardo and I grew a bond that made us inseparable. Not knowing how the CCI team knew it, but it seemed that all the dogs were perfect matches with their new lifelong families. It was remarkable watching the children's faces light up when they finally knew which canine would potentially be theirs, and when graduation came, it was the final seal of approval – along with a sloppy kiss from the new companion recognizing this is a forever deal.

Ricardo has helped to rebuild my confidence, regain my independence, and in some ways, he is a better companion than a wife. *At least he never nags me.* He can retrieve my cell phone, keys, remotes, and other items I drop on the floor. He can open and close drawers, turn lights off and on, pull doors open and push doors closed, and not only bring me my phone if I'm on the floor, but he can also lie down beside me to comfort me while we wait for assistance. He knows over forty commands. Ricardo is a Super Hero to me. He is an icebreaker for people who are shy or hesitant to meet someone in a wheelchair. Ricardo is the miracle and blessing that I've been waiting, hoping, and praying for.

> *But God will never forget the needy; the hope of the afflicted will never perish.*
>
> Psalm 9:18

Conclusion

Patience and perseverance have a magical effect before which difficulties disappear and obstacles vanish. A little knowledge that acts is worth infinitely more than much knowledge that is idle.

John Quincy Adams

THERE ARE TOO many individuals with disabilities who give up on life. I know this only too well. Life is hard, but it's also worth the fight to move forward and enjoy a fulfilling life. Those who struggle, as I have, need to know how to get through the tough times. By helping them see that life is good, I can encourage them not to let their disability define who they are, but rather use their *determination to overcome the disability* to define them.

As a young man I dreamed of becoming a professional athlete even though the odds were dramatically against me. Of the millions of people who play some type of sport, only one percent or less will become a professional athlete. After years of starting and stopping my education, I finally received my doctorate degree. Only two percent of the population will earn a doctorate degree. The percentage of doctorates for people with a disability is even smaller. In a way, by achieving a doctorate degree, I've made it to the big leagues. My dream will be fulfilled if I can now use this knowledge and experience to inspire others. Together, Ricardo and I can make a difference, be successful, and help others.

"Ricardo, if you agree with me then speak." I said.

Ricardo replied, "Bark."

I have learned a few lessons throughout my life. First, and foremost, no matter the circumstances, good or bad, God is always in control. When we focus on our difficulties, God is there to direct us on Him and the positives in our lives. If we put our problems in God's hand, He will show us the way. He has provided me with a loving family, sent strong and supporting friends, and daily strengthened me to persevere through life.

Second, when we are out of our comfort zone, God has prepared the way. On the other side of the world, I had no idea how I would survive. But God placed an army of men to help transport me from place to place without any injuries. He provided me with the confidence that I can make a difference for people with disabilities and open the eyes of their society to accept them as productive citizens.

Finally, God instilled in me at an early age the desire to succeed, the courage to try, and the ability to ask for help. I have learned that even failure can produce victory. There are two things I discovered from failure: 1) Sometimes we have to modify our goals to attain them. 2) Sometimes we fail only to discover another objective would be more desirable for us at that particular time.

I hope my story of overcoming adversities will help inspire you to do the same. We all have challenges in our lives but we need not define who we are. After triumphing over tragedies, we become stronger. By motivating each other to persevere through difficulties we demonstrate our strengths to succeed. Setting goals in life are great, but sometimes we have to re-evaluate our situations for them to happen. If we don't reach our goals it doesn't mean we have wasted our efforts. By trying to achieve our goals, even if we fail, we might be developing ourselves for other successes or other greatness. When we develop our strengths and limit our weaknesses, we can handle any circumstance that comes our way and then we can help our fellow man.

Finally: if you know someone with physical challenges, don't be afraid to offer assistance. Something as small as asking if they need help or just saying hello to recognize them as a human can mean the world to one who is confined to a wheelchair or is otherwise physically challenged. Try not to be like the preacher who said he loved me, but acted in hurtful, rather than helpful ways toward me. Even the smallest act of kindness can contribute self-worth, to a person who is trying to be successful with limitations in this world.

He gives strength to the weary and increases the power of the weak. Even youths grow tired and weary, and young men stumble and fall; but those who hope in the Lord will renew their strength. They will soar on wings like eagles; they will run and not grow weary, they will walk and not be faint. Isaiah 40:29-31

The poem below is a great guide to life. It sums up how we should encourage those we come in contact with.

Believe while others are doubting.
Plan while others are playing.
Study while others are sleeping.
Decide while others are delaying.
Prepare while others are daydreaming.
Begin while others are procrastinating.
Work while others are wishing.
Save while others are wasting.
Listen while others are talking.
Smile while others are frowning.
Commend while others are criticizing.
Persist while others are quitting.
~ **William Arthur Ward**

For more information or a speaking request:
E-mail: JamesPerdueSpeaks@comcast.net
or visit my website: JamesPerdueSpeaks.com

Printed in the USA
CPSIA information can be obtained
at www.ICGtesting.com
JSHW022358130524
62952JS00001B/46

9 781449 768683